SPECIAL SERIES NO. 10  **FEBRUARY 8, 1943**

GERMAN ANTIAIRCRAFT ARTILLERY

PREPARED BY

MILITARY INTELLIGENCE DIVISION

WAR DEPARTAMENT • WASHINGTON, DC

Published by Books Express Publishing
Copyright © Books Express, 2011
ISBN 978-1-780390-73-4

Books Express publications are available from all good retail and online booksellers. For publishing proposals and direct ordering please contact us at: info@books-express.com

MILITARY INTELLIGENCE SERVICE
WAR DEPARTMENT
WASHINGTON, February 8, 1943

SPECIAL SERIES
No. 10
MIS 461

NOTICE

1. Publication of *Special Series* is for the purpose of providing officers with reasonably confirmed information from official and other reliable sources.

2. Nondivisional units are being supplied with copies on a basis similar to the approved distribution for divisional commands, as follows:

INF DIV		CAV DIV		ARMD DIV	
Div Hq	8	Div Hq	8	Div Hq	11
Rcn Tr	2	Ord Co	2	Rcn Bn	7
Sig Co	2	Sig Tr	2	Engr Bn	7
Engr Bn	7	Rcn Sq	7	Med Bn	7
Med Bn	7	Engr Sq	7	Maint Bn	7
QM Co	7	Med Sq	7	Sup Bn	7
Hq Inf Regt, 6 each	18	QM Sq	7	Div Tn Hq	8
Inf Bn, 7 each	63	Hq Cav Brig, 3 each	6	Armd Regt, 25 each	50
Hq Div Arty	8	Cav Regt, 20 each	80	FA Bn, 7 each	21
FA Bn, 7 each	28	Hq Div Arty	3	Inf Regt	25
	150	FA Bn, 7 each	21		150
			150		

Distribution to air units is being made by the A-2 of Army Air Forces.

3. Each command should circulate available copies among its officers. Reproduction within the military service is permitted provided (1) the source is stated, (2) the classification is not changed, and (3) the information is safeguarded. Attention is invited to paragraph 10a, AR 380–5, which is quoted in part as follows: "A document * * * will be classified and * * * marked *restricted* when information contained therein is for official use only, or when its disclosure should be * * * denied the general public."

4. Suggestions for future bulletins are invited. Any correspondence relating to *Special Series* may be addressed directly to the Dissemination Branch, Military Intelligence Service, War Department, Washington, D. C.

FOREWORD

The purpose of this study is twofold: to give U. S. troops a comprehensive picture of German antiaircraft artillery and its use, and at the same time to furnish U. S. antiaircraft artillerymen data by which they can compare German methods with their own. Although some technical data is furnished for the latter purpose, it is quite obvious that a study of this type cannot include all known technical details on German antiaircraft matériel and technique.

TABLE OF CONTENTS

	Page
Section I. ORGANIZATION	1
1. General	1
2. Basic Principles of Organization	1
3. Antiaircraft as a Component of the Air Force	2
a. General	2
b. Higher units	3
(1) General	3
(2) Corps	3
(3) Division	4
(4) Regiment	4
c. The Battalion	4
(1) General	4
(2) Heavy battalion	5
(3) Mixed battalion	5
(4) Light battalion	7
(5) Reserve battalion	7
(6) Searchlight battalion	7
d. The Battery	8
(1) General	8
(2) Heavy battery	8
(3) Light and medium battery	8
(4) Searchlight battery	9
e. The Zug	10
f. Railway Flak Units	10
g. Barrage Balloon Units	11
4. Antiaircraft Organic to the Army	11
a. General	11
b. Fla Battalion	12
c. Heeresflak Abteilung	12
d. Operational Control	13
5. Antiaircraft in the Navy	13
II. WEAPONS AND EQUIPMENT	14
6. Trend of Development	14
a. Historical	14
b. Mobility	14
c. Dual-Purpose Construction	15
d. Multipurpose Use	16
e. German Classification of Flak Weapons	16

Section II. WEAPONS AND EQUIPMENT—Continued.

    7. Types of AA Guns 17
        a. *7.92-mm Standard Machine Gun* 17
            (1) *Description* 17
            (2) *Use in AA Role* 17
        b. *20-mm AA/AT Gun (Models 30 and 38)* 20
            (1) *Description* 20
            (2) *Sights* 23
            (3) *1-meter-base range-finder* 25
            (4) *Personnel* 27
        c. *20-mm Four-Barreled AA/AT Gun (Quadruple Mount)* 29
            (1) *Description* 29
            (2) *Sights* 30
        d. *37-mm AA/AT Gun* 30
            (1) *Description* 30
            (2) *Sights* 33
            (3) *Personnel* 34
        e. *40-mm AA Gun* 34
        f. *47-mm AA Gun* 35
        g. *50-mm AA/AT Gun* 35
        h. *75-mm AA Gun* 36
        i. *88-mm Dual-Purpose Gun* 37
            (1) *Development* 37
            (2) *Description* 37
            (3) *Ammunition* 41
            (4) *Fire control* 41
            (5) *Mobility* 42
            (6) *Personnel* 42
        j. *105-mm AA Gun* 43
            (1) *Description* 43
            (2) *Fire control* 44
            (3) *Personnel* 44
        k. *127-mm AA Gun* 45
        l. *150-mm AA Gun* 45
    8. Fire Control 46
        a. *Solution of the AA Fire-Control Problem* ... 46
        b. *Equipment* 46
            (1) *Kommandogerät (stereoscopic fire director)* 46
            (2) *Kommandohilfsgerät (auxiliary fire director)* 49
            (3) *Telescopic sight for 88-mm gun* 49
            (4) *Radio-location equipment* 50

Section II. WEAPONS AND EQUIPMENT—Continued.

	Page
9. SEARCHLIGHTS	51
a. Heavy Searchlights	51
(1) Equipment	51
(2) Mobility	54
(3) Personnel	54
(4) Communications	54
b. Light Searchlights	55
(1) Equipment	55
(2) Mobility	56
(3) Personnel	56
(4) Communications	56
10. BARRAGE BALLOONS	56
a. General	56
b. Description	57

III. USE OF AA WITH FIELD FORCES ... 60

	Page
11. INTRODUCTION	60
12. GENERAL PRINCIPLES	60
a. The German Task Force	60
b. Antiaircraft Task Force Allocation	61
c. Primary Missions of AA	61
d. Transition from AA Role to Other Roles	62
13. OPERATIONAL USE AGAINST AIR TARGETS	64
a. General	64
b. Protection of Columns on the March	64
(1) Panzer divisions	64
(2) Other units	66
c. Use in Forward Areas with Attacking Units	66
(1) General	66
(2) Example of use with an attacking Panzer division	67
d. Protection of Rear-Area Installations	69
e. Defense of Railway Trains	70
(1) General	70
(2) Method	70
f. Searchlights	72
g. Antiaircraft Warning System	73
14. OPERATIONAL USE AGAINST GROUND TARGETS	73
a. General	73
b. 88-mm Dual-Purpose Gun	74
(1) In antitank roles	74
(2) In other roles	75
(3) Fire-control methods	76

TABLE OF CONTENTS

Section III. USE OF AA WITH FIELD FORCES—Continued. Page

    14. OPERATIONAL USE AGAINST GROUND TARGETS—Continued.
        c. *Light and Medium Flak Guns* 77
           (1) *In an antitank role* 77
           (2) *In other roles* 77
           (3) *General* 78
    15. ESTABLISHMENT OF GUN POSITIONS 78
        a. *Heavy AA Guns* 78
           (1) *For primary AA role* 78
           (2) *For other roles* 78
        b. *Light and Medium AA Guns* 79
    16. DECEPTION AND CONCEALMENT 79

IV. USE OF AA IN DEFENSE OF GERMANY AND REAR AREAS 81

    17. HISTORICAL BACKGROUND 81
    18. GENERAL ORGANIZATION OF AA DEFENSES 81
        a. *Responsibility* 81
        b. *Defense Districts* 82
        c. *Component Arms* 84
    19. THE AA COMMAND IN AN AIR DISTRICT 84
        a. *Groups and Sub-Groups* 84
        b. *Control Centers* 85
        c. *Operational Units* 85
    20. EMPLOYMENT OF AA GUNS 86
        a. *Static Guns* 86
        b. *Use of Towers* 86
        c. *Use of Mobile Guns* 86
        d. *Use of Dummy Guns and Dummy Positions* 88
        e. *Disposition of AA Guns in Rear Areas* 88
           (1) *General* 88
           (2) *Heavy guns* 89
           (3) *Light and medium guns* 92
        f. *Fire-Control Methods* 92
           (1) *With heavy guns* 92
           (2) *With light and medium guns* 94
    21. EMPLOYMENT OF SEARCHLIGHTS 95
        a. *General* 95
        b. *Equipment* 95
        c. *Location of Searchlights* 96
           (1) *In belts* 96
           (2) *In concentrations* 96
           (3) *In gun-defended areas* 96

TABLE OF CONTENTS

Secton IV. USE OE AA IN DEFENSE OF GERMANY AND REAR AREAS—Continued.

        Page

21. EMPLOYMENT OF SEARCHLIGHTS—Continued.
    d. *Searchlight Tactics* 96
        (1) *On cloudy nights* 96
        (2) *On nights with considerable ground or industrial haze* 97
        (3) *On clear dark nights* 97
        (4) *On clear moonlight nights* 98
    e. *Dazzle and Glare* 98
22. EMPLOYMENT OF BARRAGE BALLOONS 99
23. AIRCRAFT-WARNING SYSTEM 100
    a. *Responsibility* 100
    b. *Operation* 100
    c. *Flak Intelligence Service* 101
    d. *Use of Radio-Detection Devices* 102
24. PASSIVE MEANS 102

V. CONCLUSIONS 106

ILLUSTRATIONS

Figure		Page
1.	Organization of the German mixed AA battalion	6
2.	Characteristics of German Flak weapons	18
3.	2-cm (20-mm) AA/AT gun 30 in action	20
4.	2-cm (20-mm) AA/AT gun 38 in action on self-propelled mount	21
5.	Sketch of *Linealvisier 21*	26
6.	Sighting the target with *Linealvisier 21*	27
7.	1-meter-base range-finder in use with 3.7-cm (37-mm) AA/AT gun	28
8.	2-cm (20-mm) *Flakvierling* 38 on fixed support, showing ammunition feed	31
9.	Demonstration class inspecting 3.7-cm (37-mm) AA/AT gun	32
10.	8.8-cm (88-mm) dual-purpose gun ready for action	39
11.	*Kommandogerät* in traveling position	47
12.	*Kommandogerät* ready for use	48
13.	150-cm (60-inch) standard searchlight	53
14.	German barrage balloon	58
15.	Slant-range chart	65
16.	8.8-cm (88-mm) gun in static position	87
17.	4-gun layout	90
18.	6-gun layout for coastal defense	91

Section I. ORGANIZATION

1. GENERAL

The German approach to the subject of military organization is one of extreme flexibility. The underlying thought is that in view of the rapid progress of science as applied to war, organizational practice must remain flexible if it is to take advantage promptly of new scientific development, to exploit various kinds of situations, and to cope with all types of enemies. Efficient combat effectiveness of an organization is always considered a primary requisite. It should therefore be remembered that although the organization of German antiaircraft units is founded on certain basic principles, experimentation with new tactical doctrines, economy of military manpower and equipment, or the considered needs of a task force situation may cause the organization of certain AA units to vary from normal.

2. BASIC PRINCIPLES OF ORGANIZATION

All German military organization is based on certain fundamental principles which are primarily designed to permit tactical and administrative flexibility.

One of these fundamentals is the *Einheit* (unit) principle, which provides that any given arm or service will develop a number of standard unit groups, each with standard organization, leadership, training, and equipment. The unit group is an organic entity, capable of operating independently and self-sufficient both for tactical and administrative purposes. Within a given branch or service, each basic type of unit group will represent a different combination of the various components (or weapons) of that branch or service. In AA organization the unit groups are ordinarily battalions, and the types (heavy, mixed, light, etc.) differ in organic composition with respect to their respective weapons (light and/or heavy guns, searchlights, etc.).

The *Einheit* principle of organization has several advantages. Obviously the supply and replacement of equipment can be more readily geared to a few standard types of units. The training and tactical employment of a given type of unit can be standardized, and directed with uniformity. Above all, the existence of these basic type-units, each so composed as to serve a different function, permits easy organization of any desired type of larger unit. In the AA branch, for example, regiments are formed by combining any desired number of the different basic units. And the *Einheit* system is excellently designed to facilitate the construction of task forces, made up of different amounts of necessary arms and services, in terms of the basic units of each arm or service required for a given mission.

3. ANTIAIRCRAFT AS A COMPONENT OF THE AIR FORCE

a. General

With some few exceptions, German antiaircraft units are an organic part of the German Air Force (*Luftwaffe*). German antiaircraft artillery is called *Flak-*

artillerie, and is more commonly referred to as "Flak." This term is an abbreviation of "*F*lieger- or *F*lug-*a*bwehr*k*anone," which means "cannon for defense against aviation."

Flak troops wear the uniform of the Luftwaffe, which is easily distinguished from that of the Army and Navy by the gray-blue color of the material, the lounge cut of the open collar blouse, and the plain trousers. To distinguish the AA artillery from other branches of the Air Force, red piping is worn on the cap, and the blouses of both officers and enlisted men have this distinguishing red color on the shoulder strap as lining and edging, and on the collar patches.

Flak serving in the field is fully motorized, and units intended to operate with the spearhead of the attack are equipped for cross-country operation.

Luftwaffe AA organizations and units operating with the Army are subordinated operationally and for command purposes to the Army unit concerned, and administratively (for replacements, etc.) to a parent Air Force ground unit.

b. Higher Units

(1) *General.*—In general, Flak units consist of corps, divisions, regiments, battalions, and batteries. From a practical point of view the AA corps, divisional, and regimental organizations are primarily composed of a commander, staff, and organizational troops who coordinate and assist in the disposition and activities of the basic units, the battalions (*Abteilungen*).

(2) *Corps.*—The *Flakkorps* is the highest AA unit. It may be found in rear areas or with field forces, de-

pending on the considered need for a command of this size. There is no fixed allotment of units to this highest formation; it has been noted that the corps may contain from two to four AA divisions. In general, when serving with the field forces, an AA corps would normally control the area of an army group (group of armies). It may also be found with air fleets and on some occasions with Panzer armies.

(3) *Division.*—The *Flakdivision* is frequently found in German armies. Its composition is not fixed, varying from two to five regiments. In general, when with field forces, the AA division usually operates in the area of an army.

(4) *Regiment.*—(*a*) *Pre-war establishment.*—At the outbreak of World War II, Flak regiments were organized on a standard basis of three battalions per regiment. The first two battalions were alike, each consisting of three batteries of heavy AA guns and two batteries of light AA guns with organic 60-cm (light) searchlights. The third battalion consisted of three batteries, each with nine 150-cm (heavy) searchlights.

(*b*) *Present organization.*—At the present time the composition of the regiment is flexible; it may contain from three to five battalions of any type.

c. The Battalion

(1) *General.*—The basic tactical AA unit is the battalion (*Abteilung*), which also has administrative functions. There are several known types of gun battalions, but in general these types will fall into one of three general categories consisting of heavy, mixed, and light battalions. In this connection, it should be noted that

in action the gun battalion commander is essentially a tactical commander, the battery being the fire-control unit. Allotment of AA units to Army field forces varies according to the estimated needs, but an army corps commonly has one or more separate gun battalions permanently attached to it during all operations, and at least one mixed battalion will usually be found attached to a Panzer division.

(2) *Heavy battalion.*—This battalion is equipped with either 88-mm or 105-mm antiaircraft guns, or with both, and usually consists of a headquarters with three batteries (*Batterien*) each of four, or possibly six, guns. This type of organization is rare; the unit is usually found only in static positions in Germany.

(3) *Mixed battalion.*—This is the more common type of standard battalion organization incorporating heavy AA guns. There are two separate establishments for these mixed battalions, one with four 88-mm guns per battery, the other with six. The most recent indications suggest that preference is being shown for the six-gun unit as equipment becomes available. In some cases, primarily in rear areas, 105-mm AA guns may be substituted for the 88-mm guns.

The organization of this mixed battalion (fig. 1) is as follows:

>Headquarters;
>
>3 heavy batteries, each consisting of four (possibly six) 88-mm guns, and two 20-mm guns for close protection;
>
>2 light batteries, each consisting of twelve 20-mm guns and four 60-cm (23.58-inch) search-

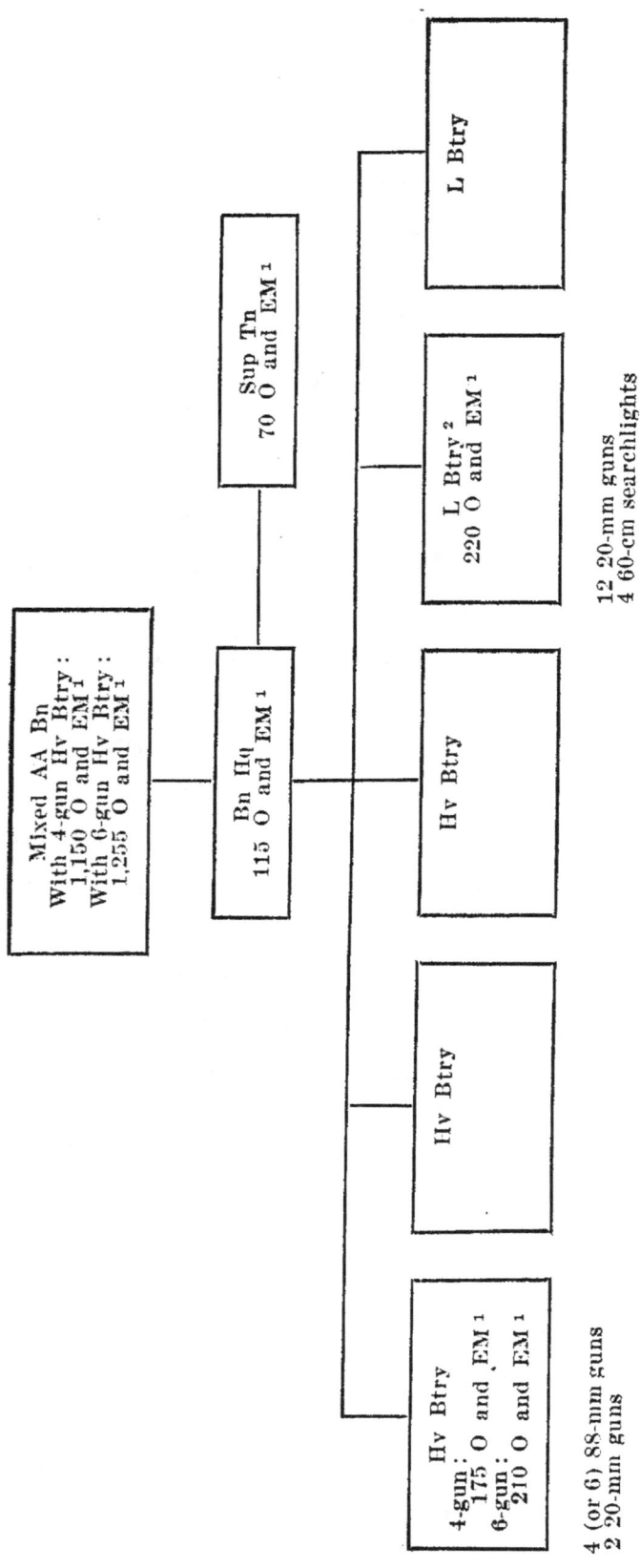

Figure 1.—Organization of the German mixed AA battalion.

lights. (A medium battery of nine 37-mm guns and four 60-cm searchlights is sometimes substituted for one of the light batteries.)

(4) *Light battalion.*—Two types of light gun battalions exist:

(*a*) Headquarters;
  3 light batteries, each of twelve 20-mm guns;
  1 searchlight battery of sixteen 60-cm searchlights.

(*b*) Headquarters;
  2 light batteries, each of twelve 20-mm guns;
  1 medium battery of nine 37-mm guns;
  1 searchlight battery of sixteen 60-cm searchlights.

(5) *Reserve battalion.*—In addition to the battalions mentioned above, there are heavy, mixed, and light reserve battalions. These have only a small amount of organic motor transport and are used in a static role in Germany and rear areas. Otherwise the reserve organization corresponds to that of standard mobile battalions. The transportation of these battalions, when necessary, is carried out by a separate transport unit.

(6) *Searchlight battalion.*—Most searchlight battalions are composed of a headquarters and three batteries, each battery containing nine 150-cm (60-inch) searchlights. Sound locators are used with these searchlights, and although their present number per battery varies with the employment of the search-

lights in rear areas, at the beginning of the war they were allotted on the basis of one per searchlight. Although mobile, most of the heavy searchlight battalions are used only within rear and static defense areas. The smaller, 60-cm (23.58-inch) lights are used with 20-mm and 37-mm AA guns, and accordingly are an organic part of both the light and mixed battalion, as mentioned above. Heavy searchlight battalions are very often grouped to form searchlight regiments, which operate as such only in rear areas.

d. The Battery

(1) *General.*—The battery (*Batterie*) is the normal fire unit of AA artillery. Several types of batteries exist:

(2) *Heavy battery.*—A heavy battery in the mixed battalion is normally organized as follows:

(*a*) Combat echelon, consisting of—

> Battery headquarters,
> Gun and instrument detachments,
> Communication detachments,
> Light Flak section,
> Ammunition detachment,
> Combat train.

(*b*) Ration transport.
(*c*) Baggage transport.

(3) *Light and medium battery.*—A light battery in a mixed battalion comprises four gun sections and one 60-cm searchlight section of four searchlights (one

searchlight is normally allotted to each gun section), and is subdivided as follows:

(*a*) Combat echelon, consisting of—

Battery headquarters,
Gun and searchlight detachments,
Communication detachment,
Ammunition detachment,
Combat train.

(*b*) Ration transport.
(*c*) Baggage transport.

(4) *Searchlight battery.*—The heavy searchlight battery is usually organized as follows:

(*a*) Combat echelon, consisting of—

Battery headquarters,
Searchlight detachments,
Communication detachment,
Combat train.

(*b*) Ration transport.
(*c*) Baggage transport.

The exact employment of the light 60-cm searchlight batteries is not known, but it is believed that the battery is subdivided into sections to permit employment of individual detachments with gun sections. This practice is somewhat similar to the system used with searchlights which are an organic part of the light gun batteries of mixed battalions. In the latter case, the four searchlights in the section are broken down into four detachments, thus allowing one light searchlight for each gun section.

e. The Zug

The closest U. S. military equivalent of the *Zug* is "platoon." It is the smallest operational unit above the single gun and ordinarily applies only to the light or medium gun platoon of three guns, although in rare cases two heavy guns may operate as a platoon. In the heavy searchlight battery, there are usually three platoons of three lights each.

f. Railway Flak Units

Antiaircraft guns are also mounted on railway cars. Railway Flak units are organized into regiments, battalions, and batteries. The precise composition of the units is not known, but it is believed that the regimental organization forms a pool from which units may be drawn as necessity arises, either for mobile defense or for train-protection purposes. Although Railway Flak units are part of the Air Force and are administered through the usual Air Force channels, it is probable that train-protection detachments are operationally subordinate to the transport authorities. There is also some evidence that AA guns provided for the defense of military trains may in certain circumstances be manned by organic Army personnel. It is interesting to note that the AA guns on railway mounts may be light or heavy, and may consist of any of the following calibers: 20-mm (single- or four-barreled), 37-mm, 75-mm (probably), 88-mm, 105-mm, and possibly even the 150-mm.

g. Barrage Balloon Units

Barrage balloon units are part of the Air Barrage Arm (*Luftsperrwaffe*), which is a branch of the Air Force. The personnel wear the uniform of the German Air Force Antiaircraft Artillery. The exact organization of current barrage balloon units is not known, mainly owing to the fact that at the outbreak of war German use of barrage balloons was on the whole still in the experimental stage, and that since that time, in accordance with German principles, the organization has varied at different places because of different needs. The best information available, however, indicates that the standard barrage balloon unit is the battalion, consisting of 3 batteries each manning about 16 balloons. In the early years of the war, the smallest unit consisted of a motorized squad of 12 men, each squad equipped with 2 balloons—one for manning and one in reserve.

4. ANTIAIRCRAFT ORGANIC TO THE ARMY

a. General

Although German AA artillery as an arm is an organic part of the Air Force, there are independent AA battalions which belong to the infantry and artillery of the Army, and are therefore organically a part of the German Army ground forces. The general term *Heeresflak* is applied to these independent units when distinguishing them, in staff tables or on orders of battle in chart form, as a category distinct from other troops, and also when referring to organic Army AA troops as distinguished from the standard Air Force AA troops. Actually, the term *Heeresflak* covers two distinct types of units: the *Flabataillon*[1] and the *Heeresflak Abteilung*. The term *Fla* is an abbreviation of "*Flugabwehr*," which means "AA defense."

b. Fla Battalion

Flabataillon troops belong to the infantry arm and wear its distinctive white piping. There are two different types of Fla battalions: the battalion of six companies in which the company apparently is the tactical unit, and the battalion of three companies in which the battalion itself is the tactical unit, although its companies may on occasion be found operating independently. The Fla battalion is equipped with standard machine guns, and either 20-mm (both single- and four-barreled) or 37-mm AA guns, all on self-propelled mounts. These guns are available for additional use in antitank or other roles against ground targets.

c. Heeresflak Abteilung

Heeresflak Abteilung troops belong to the artillery arm and wear its distinctive red piping. *Heeresflak* battalions are mechanized, and in most cases consist of three heavy batteries each of four 88-mm guns, and two light batteries each of either twelve 20-mm guns or nine 37-mm guns. All equipment may be used in AA and in antitank or other ground roles.

---

[1] The Fla "battalion" is ordinarily referred to in German military usage as *Bataillon* rather than by the more customary term *Abteilung* (see below).

d. Operational Control

The operational control of these special types of AA units is extremely flexible. Although they are normally allotted from a **GHQ** pool to an army, army corps, or division for permanent organic AA protection, they have been known to be subordinated to Luftwaffe Flak divisions and regiments.

5. ANTIAIRCRAFT IN THE NAVY

The German Navy mans AA artillery in certain coastal forts. Except for being emplaced on permanent mounts, these AA guns do not differ materially from the normal Flak armament, and the same applies to AA guns on board ships. From the point of view of organization of rear-area defenses, it should be noted that the AA armament in these coastal forts, as well as the AA guns on board Navy ships undergoing repair or at rest in harbor, is used at need as a part of the AA ground defense of the immediate area.

Section II. WEAPONS AND EQUIPMENT

6. TREND OF DEVELOPMENT

a. Historical

With the tremendous strides in development of combat aviation during the period between World War I and World War II, it became increasingly evident that a corresponding development of AA matériel and tactics was quite necessary. Although the Germans were limited in their military establishment as a result of World War I, they nevertheless conducted extensive research and tests to develop new AA matériel. During this post-war period, also, came experiments with mechanized armored vehicles, and new doctrine as to the possibilities of their employment. Under the circumstances, it was only logical that some experimentation should take place with the object of designing a gun which could be used against either aircraft or mechanized ground vehicles. In 1936 the Spanish Civil War gave the Germans a chance to test their first efforts along these lines; in 1939 the campaign in Poland permitted a full test of the refined product, and results were used as a guide on which to base standardization and further development. The later campaign in France and other campaigns have, of course, served as further proving grounds.

b. Mobility

One of the main results of the battle experiences of the Germans has been vindication of the concept that

AA guns used in any but purely static positions must be highly mobile, and that even in static situations it is to the best interests of protection against hostile aircraft to have a certain proportion of the AA artillery defenses in a highly mobile state for purposes of flexibility. Furthermore, the increased use of AA weapons with mobile units in the field has given a great spur to development of AA mobility.

c. Dual-Purpose Construction

With the practical tests of 1936 in the Spanish Civil War came the realization that with some modifications the then current AA weapons would have definite possibilities as effective antitank weapons. This finding was the more acceptable in view of the German military precept of acting on the offense wherever possible. The possibility of employing AA guns in forward areas in an offensive role definitely removed them from the status of defensive weapons and placed them in the category of important offensive weapons. The Polish Campaign, the French Campaign, and the early successes of Rommel in the Libyan Desert are eloquent proofs of the increasing development and use of AA weapons against mechanized ground targets. It should be remembered, of course, that AA gunnery demands weapons with a high rate of fire, rapid fire-control calculation, fast tracking speeds, and a high muzzle velocity. These factors contributed materially in the decision to adapt these weapons to an AT role. The original difficulty in making these AA weapons dual-purpose rested mainly in securing a satisfactory mobile carriage or mount which could withstand equally well the shock and recoil of high-elevation AA fire, and of horizontal and subhorizontal fire.

d. Multipurpose Use

With satisfactory development and use of the AA gun as an AT weapon came the logical discovery that the main AA/AT weapons could be used against targets other than aircraft or tanks. Thus we hear of the 88-mm guns being used against fortified gun positions, as well as for the direct support of ground troops, for interdiction fire against enemy communications, and for fire against river and coastal targets. We even hear of its being mounted on U-boats. As a result of these and similar experiences, German field commanders have found AA artillery to be one of their most useful weapons, and there is evidence of a trend suggesting that German artillery of the future, up to a certain caliber, will include an even greater proportion of AA weapons placed on multipurpose mounts.

e. German Classification of Flak Weapons

Although Flak weapons are generally referred to by the United Nations as light Flak and heavy Flak, probably because of the classification of AA *Abteilungen* into heavy (mixed) and light units, the Germans divide their Flak guns into the three general classifications: light, medium, and heavy. Light guns include only the various types of 20-mm Flak weapons; medium guns include the 37-mm, 40-mm, 47-mm, and reported 50-mm Flak weapons; and heavy Flak consists of the 75-mm, 88-mm, 105-mm, 127-mm, and 150-mm weapons. Of these guns, only the 20-mm, 37-mm, 88-mm, 105-mm, and 150-mm are used by the Germans to any great extent.

7. TYPES OF AA GUNS (Fig. 2)

a. 7.92-mm Standard Machine Gun

(1) *Description.*—The Germans now use one standard machine gun to fill all roles; namely, the air-cooled 7.92-mm (.31-inch) MG 34. This is considered a light machine gun when used with its light bipod, and a heavy machine gun when used with the heavy tripod mount. It is fitted in special single and dual mounts for AA purposes, and is also found in armored cars, carriers, and tanks. It fires all the types of 7.92-mm (.31-inch) ammunition which the German rifles and aircraft machine guns use. But lately there has been a marked emphasis on the use of armor-piercing ammunition in all 7.92-mm weapons. Belt feed is normally employed for the machine gun, but it is quite common for two or more 50-round belts to be joined end to end, thus reducing the delays involved in the changing of belts. A special belt drum, holding one 50-round belt compactly coiled within it, may be fitted on the left of the gun when the weapon is used as a light machine gun or for AA purposes. The gun weighs 15½ pounds without the mount. The barrel is changed after each 250 rounds of continuous fire.

(2) *Use in AA Role.*—On the AA mount, this machine gun is used organically by all branches of the German Army for local protection against low-flying aircraft. It supplements the fire furnished by rifles. Strictly speaking, this weapon is not classed as a Flak

GERMAN ANTIAIRCRAFT ARTILLERY

Weapon	20-mm AA/AT gun	20-mm 4-barreled AA/AT gun	37-mm AA/AT gun	40-mm AA gun	47-mm AA gun
German name	2-cm Flak 30 and 38.	2-cm Flakvierling 38.	3.7-cm Flak 36.	4-cm Flak 36	4.7-cm Flak 37.
Caliber (inches)	.79	.79	1.45	1.57	1.85
Muzzle velocity (foot-seconds)	2,950 (HE), 2,720 (AP).	2,950 (HE), 2,720 (AP).	2,690	2,950	2,620
Maximum horizontal range (yards)	5,230	5,230	8,744	12,300	10,350
Maximum vertical range (feet)	12,465	12,465	15,600	23,200	22,300
Effective ceiling (feet)	7,215 (with self-destroying tracer, 6 secs time of flight).	7,215 (with self-destroying tracer, 6 secs time of flight).	13,775 (with self-destroying tracer, 14 secs time of flight).	16,200	17,000
Theoretical rate of fire (rounds per minute)	280 (Model 30), 420 to 480 (Model 38).	1,680 to 1,920	150	120	25
Practical rate of fire (rounds per minute)	120 (Model 30), 180 to 220 (Model 38).	700 to 800	60	80	15
Weight of projectile	4.1 oz (HE), 5.2 oz (AP).	4.1 oz (HE), 5.2 oz (AP).	1 lb 6 oz (HE), 1 lb 8½ oz (AP).	2.2 lbs	3.3 lbs
Weight of complete round	10.6 oz (HE), 11.6 oz (AP).	10.6 oz (HE), 11.6 oz (AP).			
Weight in action	906 lbs	2,979 lbs	3,400 lbs	4,234 lbs	3,400 lbs
Weight in draught	1,650 lbs	4,866 lbs			
Elevation	−12° to +90°	−10° to +100°	−10° to +85°	−5° to +90°	−10° to +85°
Traverse	360°	360°	360°	360°	360°
Length of barrel: Calibers	65	65	50	60	
Feet or inches	4 ft 3.2 in	4 ft 3.2 in	6 ft	7 ft 10.2 in	
Remarks	Standard light Flak. Automatic, recoil-operated; single-shot or continuous fire as required; ammunition loaded in flat-box magazines containing 20 rounds; normal penetration performance with AP, 45 mm (1.77 inches) of armor at 100 yards.	Standard light Flak. Consists of four 2-cm Flak 38 guns on a quadruple mount. The magazines of 2 guns can be changed while the remaining 2 are firing.	Standard medium Flak. Automatic recoil-operated; single-shot or continuous fire as required; ammunition loaded in clips holding 6 rounds.	Bofors 1936 Model. Very few of these guns are used by the Germans.	Skoda 1937 Model. This Czech gun has apparently never been adopted by the Germans for any extensive use.

*Little information is available concerning this gun. The data shown are from German sources

Figure 2.—Characteristics

WEAPONS AND EQUIPMENT

50-mm AA/AT gun	75-mm AA gun	88-mm dual-purpose gun	105-mm AA gun	127-mm AA gun	150-mm AA gun *
5-cm Flak 41.	7.5-cm Flak L/60.	8.8-cm Flak 18 (also 36 and 38).	10.5-cm Flak 38.	12.7-cm Flak 38.	15-cm Flak 39.
1.97.	2.95.	3.46.	4.14.	5.	5.91.
	2,780.	2,755.	2,890.	2,500.	3,450.
	15,500.	16,600.	19,100.	19,600.	34,000.
	37,000.	35,700.	41,300.	42,600.	66,000.
	30,000.	34,770.	37,000.	35,000 to 40,000.	40,000 to 45,000.
	25.	25.	15.	12.	12.
	15.	12 to 15.	8 to 10.	8.	6 to 8.
	14.3 lbs.	20 lbs 1 oz (HE), 20 lbs 5 oz (HE), 21 lbs ½ oz (AP).	32 lbs 11 oz (HE).	55 lbs.	88.6 lbs.
		31 lbs 11½ oz (HE), 32 lbs (HE), 33 lbs (AP).			
	2.9 tons.	4.9 tons.	11.56 tons.		
		7.1 tons.			
	−3° to +85°.	−3° to +85°.	−3° to +87°.	−0° to +90°.	
	360°.	2 x 360°.	360°.	360°.	
	60.	56.	60.	50.	
	14 ft 9 in.	16 ft 1.8 in.	20 ft 8.4 in.	20 ft 10 in.	
Reputed to use both HE and AP. Very little authentic information is available concerning this weapon.	Krupp 1938 Model. This gun is gradually being superseded by the 8.8-cm Flak.	Standard heavy AA/AT gun for mobile use. HE shells are separately provided with both time fuze and percussion fuze. AP shells are provided with a base fuze. The firing mechanism can be set to hand, but the normal method for AA is aumatic.	Equipped with automatic fuze-setter; used mostly in a static role, although mobile versions are known to exist.	German naval AA gun. Little reliable information is available.	Dual-purpose coast defense and AA weapon, manned to a large extent by Navy personnel.

of information, and their accuracy is questionable.

of German Flak weapons.

weapon, the 20-mm cannon usually being considered the smallest caliber in the Flak class.

b. 20-mm AA/AT Gun (Models 30 and 38) (figs. 3 and 4)

(1) *Description.*—The 2-cm[2] Flak 30 (.79-inch)[3] was introduced into the German Navy in 1930 and into

Figure 3.—2-cm (20-mm) AA/AT gun 30 in action.

the German Air Force in 1935. It has been the main armament of light AA units, and can be used in an

---

[2] The German practice is to designate gun types in terms of centimeters rather than millimeters, and in all references made hereafter, the German style will be followed in the paragraphs concerned with descriptions of particular weapons.

[3] See TM-E 9-228 (German). "2-cm Flakvierling 38 (German 20-mm Antiaircraft Gun, Four-Barreled Mount)," section XII.

antitank role. The gun is fed by a flat box-magazine containing 20 rounds, and is recoil-operated. It has a detachable barrel, and is provided with automatic and single-shot mechanisms. The trigger mechanism is pedal-operated. The gun may be mounted on road or railway vehicles.

Figure 4.—2-cm (20-mm) AA/AT gun 38 in action on self-propelled mount.

It is normally transported on a single-axle trailer. This trailer may be drawn by motor transport or by horse, and is easily manhandled. The gun and its mount may also be split into loads for transport in particularly difficult country. The gun is normally fired with its mount on the ground and with the trailer removed. It can, however, be fired from the trailer in an emergency (i. e., on the march), rough traverse being obtained by pushing the trailer around.

A later version of the model 30 is contained in the 2-cm Flak 38, which does not differ materially from the earlier version apart from having higher theoretical and practical rates of fire. Particulars pertaining to the 2-cm Flak 38 are as follows:

Muzzle velocity (HE)	2,950 f/s
Muzzle velocity (AP)	2,720 f/s
Maximum horizontal range	5,230 yds
Maximum vertical range	12,465 ft
Maximum effective ceiling with self-destroying tracer ammunition.	7,215 ft with 6 secs time of flight
Theoretical rate of fire (rpm):	
(Model 30	280)
Model 38	420–480
Practical rate of fire (rpm):	
(Model 30	120)
Model 38 (estimated)	180–220
Weight in action	906 lbs
Weight in draft	1,650 lbs
Elevation	$-12°$ to $+90°$
Traverse	360°
Length of barrel	65 cals (51.2 inches)

Ammunition—three classes, as follows:

    (i) Self-destroying HE tracer with percussion fuze (weight of projectile, 4.1 ounces; weight of complete round, 10.6 ounces)

    (ii) AP tracer (weight of projectile, 5.2 ounces; weight of complete round, 11.6 ounces)

    (iii) Practice (HE and AP)

Normally the penetration performance with AP is 45 mm (1.77 inches) of armor at 100 yards.

WEAPONS AND EQUIPMENT

(2) *Sights.*—The two alternative sights normally used with the 2-cm Flak 30 are the *Flakvisier* 35 and the *Linealvisier* 21, both of which are also used with the 2-cm Flak. 38. A newer sight, known as the *Flakvisier* 38, has been developed for use with the 2-cm Flak 38.

It should be noted that all these sights are dependent on some separate continuous and accurate means of providing range. For this purpose, each gun detachment includes a range-taker who is equipped with a portable 1-meter-base stereoscopic range-finder.

In addition, a simple telescopic sight may be used with either the 2-cm Flak 30 or the 2-cm Flak 38.

(a) *Flakvisier (AA Sight) 35.*[4]—This is a reflecting-mirror sight with a computor mechanism operating on the course-and-speed principle. If the target is kept in the center of the sight, and the appropriate settings for slant range, speed, and course and angle of dive or climb are set in, then the bore of the gun is in correct alignment to pass the shell through the future position of the target. The setting for course is by means of a pointer in the horizontal plane which is kept parallel to the estimated course of the aircraft. The setting for angle of dive or climb is by means of a pointer set in the vertical plane.

(b) *Flakvisier (AA Sight) 38.*—Information about the *Flakvisier* 38 is at present very incomplete, but what is known shows that it represents a departure from the course-and-speed principle on which the *Flakvisier* 35 functions. This sight can be used both against air

---

[4] See TM-E 9-228 (German), section VII.

targets, and against moving and fixed land and sea targets.

The *Flakvisier* 38 is an electric automatic sight. The layer keeps a cross on his object glass coincident with the target, thus obtaining angle of sight and azimuth. Range, either estimated or called out by the range-taker, is set by the range-setter.

The sighting arrangement consists of illuminated cross wires automatically controlled in terms of superelevation and deflections. The elevating and traversing gears are coupled to elevating and traversing tachometer-dynamos in such a way that the voltages generated by them vary with the speeds of laying.

The gun's traversing gear is coupled to a tachometer-dynamo, which produces electric voltage varying directly with the rate of traverse. The terminals are connected to a moving coil meter which measures the strength of the electric current. A variable resistance depending on range setting is introduced, so that the current is regulated both by the tachometer-dynamo and by the strength of the range resistance. With short ranges the corresponding resistance is low and the deflection large; with long ranges, the deflection is small and the resistance high. The resultant lateral deflection is transmitted to the layer's vertical cross wire, which moves in the direction opposite to the course of the aircraft.

Vertical deflection is obtained by multiplying the rate of change of the angle of sight by the time of flight of the shell. Rate of change is measured by the rate of elevation or depression of the gun, whereas time of flight is taken as a measure of the range set. Superelevation in terms of range is added to the vertical deflection to give the appropriate quadrant elevation. The resultant value is automatically applied to the layer's horizontal cross wire.

(c) *Linealviser (Linear Sight) 21*[5] *(figs. 5 and 6)*.—This is a form of direct AA sight, giving course, speed, and range adjustment. It consists of a horizontal bar which is graduated from 0 to 1,600 meters. Range is set by turning a cylindrical hand nut on the runner of a cartwheel-type foresight, thus increasing the "lead" as the range is increased.

The ring foresight is rotatable, thus enabling course of the target to be set. A bar showing speed from 11 to 150 meters per second is mounted moveably on the foresight. This speed bar can also be adjusted to the angle of dive or climb. The backsight consists of an aperture set between two layers of nonsplintering glass inclined at 45 degrees to the horizontal bar.

Both the *Flakvisier* 35 and the *Flakvisier* 38 must be removed before the *Linealvisier* 21 can be mounted.

(d) *Telescopic sight.*—A simple telescopic sight (with a magnification of eight) may also be employed for the engagement of armored vehicles and ground targets.

(3) *1-meter-base range-finder*[6] *(fig. 7)*.—The 1-meter (39.37-inch)-base range-finder is employed by light AA detachments manning the 2-cm Flak 30 and

---

[5] See TM-E 9-228 (German), section VIII.
[6] See TM-E 9-228 (German), section IX.

38 and the 3.7-cm Flak 36. Magnification is sixfold, and the range is from 800 to 26,200 feet. This instrument is normally used strapped to the range-taker's

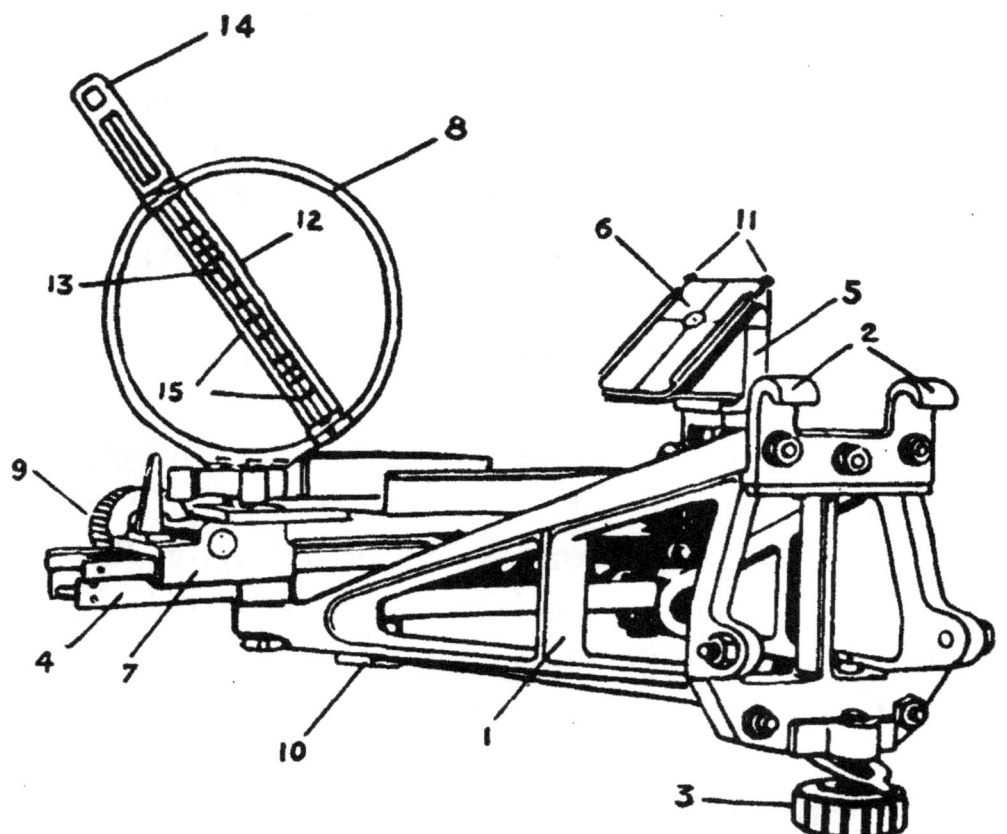

Figure 5.—Sketch of *Linealvisier* 21.

1. Bracket.
2. Suspension claws.
3. Clamping screw.
4. Slit guide.
5. Backsight bracket.
6. Backsight.
7. Slide.
8. Ring foresight.
9. Range knob.
10. Driving disk.
11. Backsight retaining springs.
12. Rule.
13. Aiming line.
14. Setting handle.
15. Speed scale.

shoulders, but there is also provision for a small tripod.

The instrument is manufactured by Carl Zeiss of Jena. It is of the standard stereoscopic pattern, estimation of distance being by means of two reticles, one in each eyepiece, which when "fused" stereoscopically appear superimposed upon the image in depth. The instrument is difficult to handle, and considerable practice is necessary before an operator can obtain satisfactory results. The operator is required to produce accurate results at slant ranges up to 4,000 meters (4,400 yards).

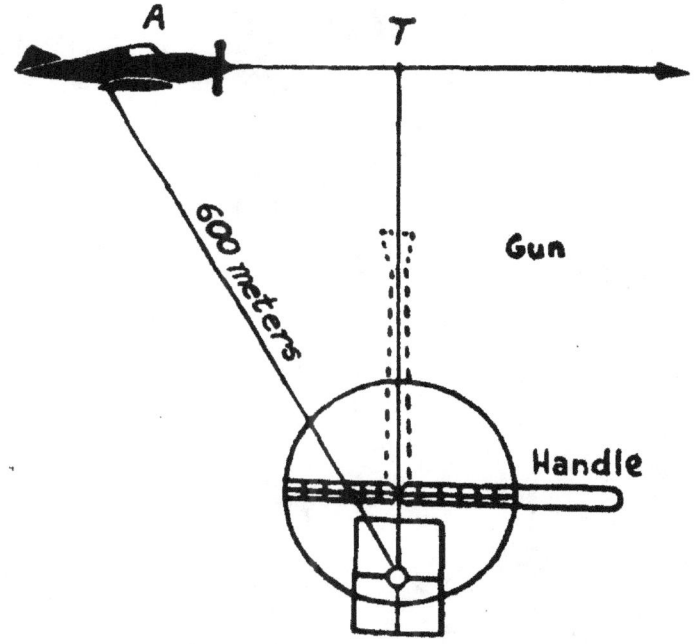

Figure 6.—Sighting the target with *Linealvisier* 21.

(4) *Personnel*.—The gun detachment consists of seven men as follows:

    Detachment Commander
    No. 1_____Layer
    No. 2_____Range-setter
    No. 3_____Course-setter
    No. 4_____Loader
    No. 5_____Range-taker
    Vehicle driver

Figure 7.—1-meter-base range-finder in use with 3.7-cm (37-mm) AA/AT gun.

c. 20-mm Four-Barreled AA/AT Gun (Quadruple Mount)[7] (Fig. 8)

(1) *Description.*—The 2-cm *Flakvierling* 38 consists of four 2-cm Flak 38 guns. It may be employed either against aerial or ground targets. It is normally transported on a special trailer, but may also be mounted on half-track vehicles or railway mounts.

There is also a static version for use on Flak towers, in coast defenses, etc. In the trailer version, the gun is normally fired with its mount on the ground and with the trailer removed. It can, however, be fired from the trailer in an emergency (i. e., on the march). A traverse of only about 10 degrees at top elevation is possible in this position. Two foot-levers operate the trigger mechanism. Each foot-lever actuates the triggers of two diametrically opposite guns (i. e., the top left and the bottom right, and the top right and bottom left). This arrangement provides uninterrupted, continuous fire. While two guns are firing, the magazines of the other two can be changed. When both firing levers are operated, all four guns fire simultaneously. Furthermore, should there be a stoppage on one or more guns, the remaining guns can continue to fire. Provision is made for single-shot or continuous fire on each weapon. A shield may be fitted to the carriage. This weapon fires the same ammunition as does the 2-cm Flak 38 described above.

The following additional characteristics pertain to the four-barreled mount:

---

[7] See TM–E 9–228 (German).

Theoretical rate of fire	1,680–1,920 rpm
Practical rate of fire (estimated)	700–800 rpm
Elevation	−10° to +100°
Traverse	360°
Rate of traverse (two speed)	7½° or 22½° (per turn of handwheel)
Rate of elevation (two speed)	4° or 12° (per turn of handwheel)
Loading	By flat box-magazines containing 20 rounds in two staggered rows
Weight in action (mobile version)	2,979 lbs
Weight in draft (with accessories)	4,866 lbs
Weight of trailer 52	1,848 lbs
Weight in action (static version)	1.25 tons

(2) *Sights.*—The equipment is provided with the *Flakvisier* 40 (or, where not available, *Linealvisier* 21—see b (2) (c), above), and a telescopic sight for the engagement of ground targets (see b (2) (d), above). The *Flakvisier* 40 operates on the same principle as the *Flakvisier* 38, described in b (2) (b), above. Apparently, *Flakvisier* 35 may also be used on the 2-cm *Flakvierling* 38.

d. 37-mm AA/AT Gun (figs. 7 and 9)

(1) *Description.*—The 3.7-cm (1.45-inch) Flak 36 is the smallest caliber of medium Flak artillery. This gun is mounted on a two-wheeled trailer, detached when the gun is in the firing position, but the gun can be fired from the trailer in an emergency. This method can be adopted both in an AT and an AA role on the march; movement in azimuth is, however, very limited under these conditions, and the crew may have to move the gun and trailer bodily to enable the target to be engaged.

Figure 8.—2-cm (20-mm) *Flakvierling* 38 on fixed support, showing ammunition feed.

Figure 9.—Demonstration class inspecting 3.7-cm (37-mm) AA/AT gun. (The German instructor is pointing to the feed mechanism.)

WEAPONS AND EQUIPMENT

When on the trailer, the gun is towed behind motor transportation in which the personnel and stores are also carried. This gun also is found on self-propelled half-track vehicles and on railway mounts. Other characteristics of this gun are as follows:

Muzzle velocity	2,690 f/s
Maximum horizontal range	8,744 yds
Maximum vertical range	15,600 ft
Theoretical rate of fire	150 rpm
Practical rate of fire	60 rpm
Maximum effective ceiling with self-destroying tracer ammunition. (A new shell has been introduced, which is self-destroying at 9,185–11,480 ft after 7–10 secs.)	13,775 ft with 14 secs time of flight
Automatic, recoil-operated; the firing mechanism can be set for single-shot or continuous fire as required. The ammunition is loaded in clips holding 6 rounds.	
Weight in action	3,400 lbs (approx.)
Elevation	−10° +85°
Traverse	360°
Length of barrel	50 cals (6 ft)

Ammunition—two classes, as follows:
 (i) Self-destroying HE tracer with percussion fuze (weight of projectile, 1 lb. 6 oz)
 (ii) AP tracer (weight of projectile, 1 lb 8½ oz)

(2) *Sights.*—The *Flakvisier* 33 is normally used for AA fire with this weapon. This sight is believed to be similar in principle to the *Flakvisier* 35 used with the 2–cm Flak 30, described above. Observation by tracer is used with this sight for close targets where the angular velocity is high; in such cases, only the course is set into the sight.

(3) *Personnel.*—The gun detachment consists of 12 men as follows:

Detachment Commander
No. 1_____ Layer
No. 2_____ Range-setter
No. 3_____ Course-setter
No. 4_____ Loader
No. 5_____ Range-taker
No. 6_____ ⎱ Ammunition numbers
No. 7_____ ⎰
Vehicle driver
Vehicle driver's relief
Spotters (2)

e. 40-mm AA Gun

Although used by the Germans, the 4-cm (1.57-inch) Flak 36 is not encountered very often in German AA units. The few guns known to be in the hands of the Germans are believed to have been taken for the most part from the Polish Army after the Polish Campaign. The 4-cm Flak 36 is a Bofors gun, having characteristics similar to the weapon used by the British except for some few variations in performance characteristics. A few characteristics of this gun are as follows:

Muzzle velocity	2,950 f/s
Maximum horizontal range	12,300 yds
Maximum vertical range	23,200 ft
Effective ceiling	16,200 ft
Theoretical rate of fire	120 rpm
Practical rate of fire	80 rpm
Weight of projectile	2.2 lbs
Weight in action	4,234 lbs
Elevation	$-5°$ to $+90°$
Traverse	360°
Length of barrel	60 cals

WEAPONS AND EQUIPMENT

f. 47-mm AA Gun

The 4.7-cm Flak 37 has in the past been used to some extent by the Germans as a medium AA/AT gun, but there are indications that the Germans are not entirely satisfied with its performance, and that no attempt will be made to produce this gun in any large quantity. This weapon is a Czech model, having originally been produced at the Skoda works and adopted for use by the Czechoslovakian Army. The gun is tractor-drawn, but it is also found on some self-propelled mounts. A few of the characteristics are as follows:

Muzzle velocity	2,620 f/s
Maximum horizontal range	10,350 yds
Maximum vertical range	22,300 ft
Maximum effective ceiling	17,000 ft
Theoretical rate of fire	25 rpm
Practical rate of fire	15 rpm
Weight in action	3,400 lbs (approx.)
Elevation	−10° to +85°
Traverse	360°
Weight of projectile	3.3 lbs

g. 50-mm AA/AT Gun

The 5-cm Flak 41 (1.97-inch) has only recently been brought into service. Its introduction indicates a considered need for a medium gun with a higher ceiling and greater destructive power than the standard medium 3.7-cm. No detailed or accurate information is available about its performance, but it is claimed by the Germans to fire both HE and AP ammunition and to be provided with a new Flak sight 41, which, according to a sketchy German report, is operated by one man and is a completely automatic clockwork-sight. Also according to the report, range is introduced and angular velocities are calculated in such a way that superelevation and vertical and lateral deflections are automatically applied.

This reported new gun should not be confused with the 5-cm Pak[8] 41, which is purely an AT weapon.

h. 75-mm AA Gun

The 7.5-cm Flak L/60 is a 1938 model, and is only slightly modified from the 7.5-cm Flak L/59, which is a 1934 model. The 7.5-cm Flak L/60 is carried on a trailer mount and is ordinarily tractor-drawn. Some versions of this gun may also be found on self-propelled mounts, and in fixed AA installations. The weapon is not used to any great extent, however, since the 88-mm gun has become the standard German gun of this class, just as the U. S. 90-mm AA gun is superseding the U. S. 3-inch AA gun. Some of the characteristics of the 7.5-cm Flak L/60 are as follows:

Muzzle velocity	2,780 f/s
Maximum horizontal range	15,500 yds
Maximum vertical range	37,000 ft
Maximum effective ceiling	30,000 ft
Theoretical rate of fire	25 rpm
Practical rate of fire	15 rpm
Weight in action	2.9 tons
Elevation	−3° to +85°
Traverse	360°
Length of barrel	60 cals
Weight of projectile	14.3 lbs

---

[8] *Pak* is an abbreviation of "*Panzerabwehrkanone*," which means "antitank gun."

i. 88-mm Dual-Purpose Gun (figs. 10 and 16)

(1) *Development.*—The German 8.8-cm gun was introduced in 1934 as the standard mobile AA gun. It was then known as the 8.8-cm Flak 18. In 1936, during the Spanish War, it proved a very effective weapon against tanks, which were at that time relatively lightly armored. In order to develop still further this dual-purpose employment, the Germans produced armor-piercing ammunition for the weapon, a telescopic sight suitable for the engagement of ground targets, and a more mobile carriage; an HE shell with a percussion fuse was also produced so that the weapon could, when necessary, be employed in a field-artillery role.

The improved equipment was ready in time for the Battle of France, when it proved itself capable of dealing with the heavier French tanks, against which the then standard AT gun, the 3.7-cm (1.45-in) Pak, was relatively ineffective. The next step was to provide the gun with a new carriage, from which the gun could engage tanks without being taken off its wheels, and to fit a shield. Still more recently, a self-propelled mount has been reported; and while there is no precise information as to its design, it appears that from this mount the gun can readily take on ground, but not air, targets.

(2) *Description.*—(*a*) *General.*—For all practical purposes, the operating characteristics of the 18, 36, and 38 models of this weapon are the same. The main characteristics of the 8.8-cm Flak 18 are as follows:

Muzzle velocity	2,755 f/s
Maximum horizontal range	16,600 yds
Maximum vertical range	35,700 ft
Maximum effective ceiling	34,770 ft
Theoretical rate of fire	25 rpm
Practical rate of fire	12 to 15 rpm
Weight in action	4.9 tons
Weight in draft	7.1 tons
Elevation	$-3°$ to $+85°$
Traverse	360° (limited to two complete revolutions of the handwheels, either side of zero, to avoid excessive twisting of the data transmission cable)
Length of barrel	56 cals

(*b*) *Gun data (8.8-cm Flak 18).*—The gun consists of a jacket, a sleeve, a removable tube in three sections, and a breech ring. The three-section tube is held in place by the breech ring in the rear and by a locking collar in the front, both of which are secured to the sleeve. The sleeve is secured to the jacket by a locking ring at the breech end. One of the joints in the three-section liner is in the chamber of the gun and is therefore sealed by the shell case, but the other occurs at about one-third of the distance to the muzzle.

The breech mechanism is of the horizontal sliding-wedge type, semiautomatic and self-cocking. As the gun recoils, the mechanism opens, ejects the empty case, and at the same time, compresses the striker and breechblock operating springs. Loading is by automatic rammer used in conjunction with a loading tray.

Figure 10.—8.8-cm (88-mm) dual-purpose gun in action.

Firing is by percussion. The withdrawal of the loading tray will operate the firing mechanism unless set to "Hand." The breechblock may be opened and closed by hand if desired. The mechanism must be hand-operated for loading the first round. Safety arrangements are incorporated in the mechanism to prevent firing until the breech is in the closed position.

(c) *Mount data.*—The mount has a platform which rests squarely on the ground when the gun is in the firing position. The platform has four legs, with jacks at the outer ends of each for approximate leveling. In the traveling position, the two side legs fold upward. The pedestal is secured to the platform and supports the body through a gimbal ring and body pivot housing. The body, which contains the azimuth and elevation gears, supports the cradle on its trunnions and rotates in the housing for azimuth traverse. Accurate cross-leveling is accomplished by rocking the body pivot housing in the gimbal ring by means of cross-leveling handwheels on the platform. A 5-degree movement is possible by this means.

The gun slides on the cradle, to which it is connected through the recoil mechanism. The recoil system incorporates a hydraulic buffer below the barrel, and a hydro-pneumatic recuperator above. Both cylinders are secured to the cradle, and the pistons are connected to the breech ring. The buffer contains 18.8 pints of buffer fluid. The recuperator contains about 4½ gallons of fluid and an approximately equal volume of air at 39 atmospheres. Length of recoil is variable, being about 1,050 mm at 0 degrees quadrant elevation, and

WEAPONS AND EQUIPMENT 41

700 mm at 85 degrees quadrant elevation. The automatic rammer operates with the return cylinder, loading tray, and actuating mechanism. The internal construction of the return cylinder resembles that of the recuperator on a smaller scale.

A hand-operated fuze-setter with two openings is fitted to the left side of the body.

To put the gun in traveling position, the side legs are folded upward and secured. A limber and carriage are attached to the platform, which is raised by winches and secured. Some modifications of this gun are capable of being fired from the traveling position at ground targets, and there is also a model on a self-propelled mount.

(3) *Ammunition.*—The three types of ammunition used with this weapon are as follows:

Type	Weight of complete round	Length of complete round	Weight of projectile	Fuze
HE shell	31 lbs 11½ oz	36.39 in	20 lbs 1 oz	Time-clockwork.
HE shell	32 lbs	36.69 in	20 lbs 5 oz	Nose percussion.
AP tracer	33 lbs	34.21 in	21 lbs ½ oz	Base.

Penetration of the AP projectile against homogeneous armor plate is approximately as follows:

Thickness of plate
Range in yards   *Normal*   *30°*
1,000 -- 4.7 in   4.1 in
1,500 -- 4.2 in   3.7 in
2,000 -- 3.7 in   3.1 in

(4) *Fire control.*—The gun may be laid on the target by three methods:

(a) Indirect laying, by matching the pointers of the

data receivers, which are controlled by the director (*Kommandogerät* No. 36, described in par. 8 b (1), below).

(b) Direct laying, by means of the Flak ZF 20–E telescopic sight. Vertical and lateral deflections are applied to the telescope, and the man at the azimuth handwheel puts the cross hairs on the target. The gun is elevated by the man on the elevation handwheel, who follows an indicating arm which moves with the sight.

(c) The dial sight may be used for laying the gun in azimuth, while the quadrant elevation is set in by the elevation man as ordered.

(5) *Mobility.*—This gun is normally towed by two types of half-track vehicles. These vehicles, which are respectively of 140 and 185 horsepower and weigh 11½ and 14½ tons loaded, carry the gun crew, as well as a supply of ammunition in lockers at the rear of the vehicle. The exact amount of ammunition carried is not known, but seems to be at least about 35 rounds.

(6) *Personnel.*—(a) *For action against aircraft.*—The gun detachment consists of a detachment commander and nine men, with duties for antiaircraft action as follows:

```
Detachment Commander
No. 1_____  Elevation-setter
No. 2_____  Azimuth-setter
No. 3_____  Loading and firing number
No. 4⎫
No. 5⎭ _____  Ammunition numbers
No. 6_____  Fuze-setter
No. 7⎫
No. 8⎬ _____  Ammunition numbers
No. 9⎭
```

WEAPONS AND EQUIPMENT

(b) *For action against ground targets.*—For the engagement of ground targets, the duties of this gun detachment are as follows:

```
Detachment Commander
No. 1_____Elevation-setter
No. 2_____Azimuth-setter
No. 3_____Loading and firing number
No. 4⎫
No. 5⎪
No. 6⎬_____Ammunition numbers
No. 7⎭
No. 8_____Range-setter
No. 9_____Lateral-deflection setter
```

j. 105-mm AA Gun

(1) *Description.*—The 10.5-cm Flak 38 (4.14-inch) is being encountered in increasing numbers. Although the 8.8-cm gun, because of its success and in particular its value as a dual-purpose weapon, is likely to remain the main armament of heavy Flak, it is known that the 10.5-cm gun ranks high on German priorities for war production. The possibility that this larger weapon may be developed as an AA/AT gun must, therefore, be reckoned with. It is noteworthy that a new tractor-drawn mobile version was produced some time ago, although it is reported that the mount proved unsatisfactory.

Some of the main characteristics of this weapon are as follows:

Muzzle velocity	2,890 f/s
Maximum horizontal range	19,100 yds
Maximum vertical range	41,300 ft
Maximum effective ceiling	37,000 ft

Theoretical rate of fire................................ 15 rpm
Practical rate of fire.................................. 8 to 10 rpm
Weight in action....................................... 11.56 tons
Elevation.. —3° to +87°
Traverse... 360°
Length of barrel....................................... 60 cals

Ammunition—three classes, as follows:

 (i) HE with time fuze (weight of projectile, 32 lbs 11 oz)
 (ii) HE with percussion fuze (weight of projectile, not known)
 (iii) AP with base fuze (weight of projectile, not known)

An automatic fuze-setter is used with the gun, but it is not known whether it operates on the same principles as does the fuze-setter fitted on the 8.8-cm weapon. Details of the loading and firing mechanism are not known, but they are probably substantially the same as for the 8.8-cm gun.

(2) *Fire control.*—The *Kommandogerät* No. 40 is employed with this gun for firing at aircraft. A description of the *Kommandogerät* No. 36, which is used with the 8.8-cm gun, is given in a later portion of this study (see par. 8b (1), below). It is believed that the No. 40 operates on the same principle as the No. 36. In addition, the *Kommandohilfsgerät* No. 35 (auxiliary predictor) can also be used with this gun. A description of the latter instrument appears elsewhere in this study.

(3) *Personnel.*—Except for additional men that might be required to handle the heavier ammunition, the personnel comprising the gun detachment is substantially the same as for the 8.8-cm weapon.

k. 127-mm AA Gun

The 12.7-cm Flak 38 (5-inch) is a naval AA weapon. Although this gun is known to be used by the Germans, mainly in a static AA role in Germany, little reliable data is available concerning its characteristics and operation. Its known main characteristics are as follows:

Muzzle velocity	2,500 f/s
Maximum horizontal range	19,600 yds
Maximum vertical range	42,600 ft
Maximum effective ceiling	35,000 to 40,000 ft
Theoretical rate of fire	12 rpm
Practical rate of fire	8 rpm
Elevation	0° to 90°
Traverse	360°
Weight of projectile	55 lbs
Length of barrel	50 cals

l. 150-mm AA Gun

The 15-cm Flak 39 (5.91-inch) is used by the Germans in a dual-purpose role, for AA and coast defense. For the most part it is found on fixed mounts in static roles, manned to a large extent by Navy personnel. Little accurate information is available on this gun, but the following limited data will serve to give some indication of its capabilities:[9]

Muzzle velocity	3,450 f/s
Maximum horizontal range	34,000 yds
Maximum vertical range	66,000 ft
Maximum effective ceiling	40,000 to 45,000 ft
Theoretical rate of fire	12 rpm
Practical rate of fire	6 to 8 rpm
Weight of projectile	88.6 lbs

---

[9] The data is from German sources and cannot be adequately verified.

8. FIRE CONTROL

a. Solution of the AA Fire-Control Problem

There is no indication that a director of any type is ordinarily used with the light and medium Flak guns, the Germans apparently having decided that the development of the Flak sights already described is more profitable and practicable than the development of directors. For use with heavy guns, the German development of fire-control apparatus is strikingly similar to our own. They have an older, angular-speed director which is used for auxiliary purposes, but the latest and most commonly used instrument operates on the linear-speed method, using present azimuth, present angular height, and present slant range as basic elements.

b. Equipment

(1) *Kommandogerät (stereoscopic fire director)* (figs. 11 and 12).—(a) *Description.*—This fire-control instrument combines into one instrument a 4-meter-base Zeiss stereoscopic height- and range-finder, and a director. Two types are known: the No. 36, employed with the 8.8-cm Flak gun, and the No. 40, employed with the 10.5-cm Flak gun. The principles and method of operation of the No. 40 are not known, but they are probably similar to those of the No. 36, details of which follow.

(b) *Method of operation.*—The stages in the production of the firing data in the No. 36 are as follows:

(1) The height- and range-finder furnishes present

azimuth, angle of sight, and slant range to the target, all of which may be termed initial data.

(2) The rate of change, obtained by continuously feeding this data into the predictor, provides the horizontal ground speed and the course angle of the target, which may be termed intermediate data.

Figure 11.—*Kommandogerät* in traveling position.

(Note that the range-finder is carried separately.)

(3) The combination of initial and intermediate data provides the vertical and lateral deflection and range correction to determine the future position. From this combination, the gun data is obtained by mechanical computation within the predictor.

(c) *Transmission of data to guns.*—The gun data thus obtained (in terms of firing azimuth, quadrant elevation, and fuze) are normally transmitted electrically to the guns, in the following manner: each of the three receiver dials at the gun (i. e., for firing azimuth, quadrant elevation, and fuze) is provided with three mechanical pointers pivoted at the center of the dial. There are three concentric circles on the dial, each with 10 holes numbered from 0 to 9, each hole being fitted with an electric bulb. The outer circle represents units; the center, tens; and the inner, hundreds. The

Figure 12.—*Kommandogerät ready for use.*

appropriate bulbs light up in accordance with the data transmitted from the *Kommandogerät*. The actual value of the reading is different for each dial, the unit (i. e., on the outer circle) in each instance having the following values:

Azimuth receiver	0.36°
Elevation receiver	0.10°
Fuze receiver	0.5 (of the German system of fuze range) [10]

---

[10] The German fuze scale reads from 0 to 350, the numerals being reference numbers which indicate definite times of flight.

These figures provide a measure of the limits of accuracy obtained in transmission. The two gun-layers and the fuze-setter bring their mechanical data pointers into coincidence (covering the illuminated bulbs with the transparent celluloid ends of the pointers) by manually actuating azimuth and elevation handwheels on the guns, and the fuze-setting handwheel on the machine fuze-setter.

(2) *Kommandohilfsgerät (auxiliary fire director).*—This instrument is used for auxiliary purposes, and operates on the principle of calculation of the rates of change of angular velocity. A separate 4-meter-base stereoscopic height- and range-finder provides the present slant range to the target, and this data is passed orally to the director. By following the target continuously for azimuth and elevation, and by setting in range continuously, the rates of change of azimuth, elevation, and slant range are obtained. These, multiplied by time of flight, give the lateral and vertical deflections and a correction for range. These corrections, applied to the present data, provide future data which are corrected for abnormal ballistic conditions, dead time, and drift, and which are then passed to the guns as gun azimuth, quadrant elevation, and fuze. Data in this case are transmitted to the guns by telephone, no electrical transmission being provided.

(3) *Telescopic sight for 88-mm gun.*—The 8.8-cm gun is fitted with a telescopic sight primarily for the engagement of ground targets; the latest type is the telescopic sight 20-E (ZF 20-E). It weighs about 10 pounds and is a monocular type with a magnification

of four and a field view of 17.5 degrees. The reticle is made with two cross lines interrupted at the center to form a laying mark, an arrangement which is usual in German instruments. There is a range drum graduated in hundreds from 0 to 9,400 meters, and a superelevation drum with graduations of 1/16 of a degree, from 0° to 12°. There are also lateral- and vertical-deflection drums.

For AT use, the lateral- and vertical-deflection drums are set to zero. Range is set on the range drum, thereby automatically applying the necessary superelevation. Corrections from observation of fire are applied to deflection drums as required.

An older type of instrument, the 2F 20, may be fitted. This has the same particulars, but no range drum; superelevation must be found from a range table and applied.

(4) *Radio-location equipment.*—It is known that German radio-location equipment for fire-control data is being produced on a high priority, and there is no doubt that this will constitute a most important line of future development. This activity is taking place parallel to the development of radio-detection equipment for warning against hostile aircraft. Aerial observers flying over gun positions in Germany and the gun-defended portions of occupied European countries have reported seeing instruments, identified as German radio-location instruments, in close proximity to gun positions. This would indicate that these radio-location instruments are being used with gun batteries, probably as a means of furnishing early basic data to

the directors. Another possible use of these instruments is to furnish early information for calculation of data for barrage and deterrent fire.

9. SEARCHLIGHTS

a. Heavy Searchlights

(1) *Equipment.*—(a) *General.*—The equipment used with a heavy searchlight consists of four main units: a sound locator, the searchlight, an optical director, and the generator. Beyond the introduction of remote control, little is known of recent developments in German searchlight equipment. Some searchlights of 200-cm, or larger, diameter have been developed, and the sound locator has possibly been improved by the introduction of some form of electrical amplification. The standard heavy searchlight, however, is the 150-cm (60–inch) size. Information from radio-location equipment is almost certainly passed to the searchlights, but the extent and method of its application are unknown.

(b) The ring-trumpet sound locator derives its name from the construction of the four trumpets or horns as a single unit of ring shape. Ordinary stethoscopic listening by two listeners, one for azimuth and one for elevation, is employed. The base length is 135 cm (53.1 inches), giving a theoretical accuracy of about one-half degree. In average weather conditions, the range is about 6,600 yards. The trumpets can be moved through 360° in azimuth and from 0° to 108° in elevation. The "lag calculator" is in the base of the sound locator. Estimated target and sound speeds (the latter based on weather conditions) are set into the lag calculator, which continuously reconstructs the triangle formed by the line of sound reception, the line of sight (present position), and the target course. The azimuth and elevation of the line of sight are shown electrically both at the sound locator and at the searchlight. The sound locator and the searchlight are connected by a cable.

(c) The 150-cm (60-inch) searchlight (fig. 13) has a glass parabolic reflector of 150-cm diameter. The focal length is 650 mm. The high-current-density arc lamp is self-regulating and is fitted in an inverted position in the projector barrel. The light is of 990 million candle power and has a range in favorable weather of 8,800 yards at a height of 13,000 to 16,500 feet. The current consumption is 200 amperes at 77 volts. The projector can be moved in azimuth through 360°, and in elevation from $-12°$ through the vertical to $-12°$ on the other side. The movement of the projector in azimuth is by means of a control arm, which is normally manipulated by hand; its movement in elevation is by means of either of two handwheels, one on the control arm and one on the opposite side of the projector. Electrical receivers for azimuth and elevation show the azimuth and elevation of the line of sight calculated by the sound locator. The beam is exposed and covered by a shutter of Venetian-blind type. More recent models are believed to be equipped with azimuth and elevation driving-motors which can be operated by automatic remote control from the sound locator or from the optical director; the exposing and covering of the beam on these models is controlled from the optical director. It is understood that the driving motors have three or four speeds, 1 degree and/or 1.5, 4, and 16 degrees per second.

Figure 13.—150-cm (60-inch) standard searchlight.
(The elevation receiver is on the side of the drum near the extended hand control, and the azimuth receiver is in the rear.)

(d) The optical director consists of a pair of night glasses of ample magnification mounted on a tripod. The director is fitted with an overhead, open sight and with scales showing the azimuth and elevation to which the night glasses are pointing. When employed with remote-control equipment, it is believed that the optical director is located 30 to 45 yards from the searchlight, thus becoming in effect a control station.

(e) The searchlight generator is driven by an 8-cylinder internal-combustion engine which develops 51 horsepower at 1,500 revolutions per minute. The 24-kilowatt generator gives a direct current of 200 amperes at 110 volts at 1,500 revolutions per minute. The cable to the searchlight projector is 220 yards long.

(2) *Mobility.*—The sound locator, searchlight, and generator are each mounted on a detachable four-wheeled trailer of standard pattern, towed by a truck. Each section or unit therefore requires three trucks for transportation purposes.

(3) *Personnel.*—The individual searchlight section is composed of 14 individuals with duties as follows:

```
Section Commander
No. 1_____ Searchlight layer for elevation
No. 2_____ Searchlight controller and layer for azimuth
No. 3_____ Lamp attendant
No. 4_____ Optical director spotter
No. 5_____ Generator attendant
No. 6_____ Engine attendant
No. 7_____ Lag-calculator operator
No. 8_____ Azimuth listener
No. 9_____ Elevation listener
No. 10_____ Sound locator spotter
3 truck drivers
```

(4) *Communications.*—Field telephones are the normal means of communication, each battery having three telephone-erection parties, with sufficient equipment to connect the searchlight sections to platoon headquarters, which, in turn, are connected to battery headquarters.

Communications with battalion headquarters are also normally by telephone. Each battery has one small truck equipped with voice radio for communication with the battalion, and two details with pack voice-radio for use within the battery as required.

b. Light Searchlights

(1) *Equipment.*—(a) *General.*—The equipment consists of a 60-cm (23.50-inch) searchlight and a generator. This highly mobile and easily handled equipment, designed for use without a sound locator against low-flying targets, appears to have given satisfaction in the limited role for which it was intended. There are no indications that any changes in the design are contemplated.

(b) The 60-cm (23.58-inch) searchlight has a glass parabolic reflector of 60-cm diameter. The focal length is 250 mm. The high-current-density arc lamp is self-regulating and is fitted in an inverted position in the projector barrel. The light is of 135 million candle power and has a range (in focus) in favorable weather of 5,700 yards at a height of 5,000 feet; with dispersed beam the range is 3,500 yards. The current consumption is 90 amperes at 60 volts. The projector is moved in azimuth and elevation by handwheels operated by the searchlight controller, who is seated behind the projector barrel. The beam is exposed and covered by a shutter of Venetian-blind type.

(c) An 8-kilowatt searchlight generator gives the required current at 85 volts. It is connected to the searchlight by a cable 110 yards long.

(2) *Mobility.*—The projector is mounted on a detachable two-wheeled trailer, towed by a truck. The same truck carries the generator, which can either be operated in the body of the truck or be unloaded on the ground.

(3) *Personnel.*—The individual searchlight section is composed of five individuals with duties as follows:

```
Section Commander
No. 1------------------ Searchlight controller
No. 2------------------ Lamp attendant
No. 3------------------ Generator attendant
Truck driver
```

No. 1 lays the searchlight as ordered, and puts the light into action with a dispersed beam. The section commander gives directional orders and orders a search, if required. The search is carried out in S-shape light-tracks across the target course. If No. 1 gets on target, No. 2 puts the beam in focus. No. 1 shuts off the beam on the section commander's orders.

(4) *Communications.*—Since light searchlights normally operate directly with light-gun platoons, the light-searchlight section from the communication point of view is normally serviced by the light Flak battery or platoon with which the light-searchlight section is operating.

10. BARRAGE BALLOONS

a. General

Although no extensive use of barrage balloons was contemplated by the Germans before the beginning of World War II, subsequent developments proved that barrage balloons have a definite psychological value as well as a practical value, and experiments conducted prior to the outbreak of the war were very soon put into practical use over strategic manufacturing centers in western Germany.

As in the U. S. Army and in the British Isles, the main purpose of the German barrage balloon is to hold a steel cable suspended vertically in the air. Thus, below the operating height of the balloon, this cable obstacle presents both a physical and mental hazard to enemy pilots attempting to enter that space. It is of course axiomatic that the type of balloon used for this purpose will be strong enough to suspend the cable, and that the balloon is designed in accordance with sound aeronautical principles (i. e., in terms of streamlining, capacity to resist wind stress, etc.). The extent of engineering developments of the German barrage balloon since the beginning of World War II is not definitely known, but it is believed that any changes effected consist only of minor modifications of the types in existence at the beginning of the war.

b. Description (fig. 14)

At the beginning of World War II, there were two general types of barrage balloons in existence in Germany. Both types were egg-shaped and had four fins at the tail end: a top fin, two side fins, and a bottom fin. The top fin and two side fins were inflated with air. The bottom fin was called the steering sack and had an opening at both ends. When the balloon was up, air entered the bottom opening of the fin and made its exit through the top opening. The fins (and especially the bottom fin) served to keep the balloon in proper position with respect to the wind and air currents. When inflated, the shape of the balloon could be likened to a short fat cigar, with a tail like a Japanese goldfish. Rubber cords were fastened tightly around the outside of the inflated balloon to assist in keeping its shape and strength.

Figure 14.—German barrage balloon.

Although both types of balloons were inflated with hydrogen gas, they differed in that one type was inflated exclusively with hydrogen gas while the second was inflated with both hydrogen gas and air, each being in separate chambers. At least the first type, and probably both types, were divided into six gas chambers. The second type had its air compartment behind the hydrogen gas compartment, the air being forced out through air valves as the gas expanded at higher altitudes. As both types were still more or less in the experimental stage, they varied in size, the largest being approximately 60 feet long and 25 feet in diameter, with a long "flutter" tail. Although various types of lethal devices were in the process of experimentation, the final decision along these lines is not known.

Section III. USE OF AA WITH FIELD FORCES

11. INTRODUCTION

A discussion of the war-time use of AA artillery by the Germans falls into two general classifications: use with the field forces and use in defense of Germany and other static rear-area objectives. In this classification, however, it should be remembered that German tactical doctrine holds that organizations and weapons should not be placed in a purely defensive role except where the tactical situation absolutely demands such disposition. Wherever possible, an offensive plan will always take precedence over a plan which is purely defensive. Thus, even in rear-area and static positions, the German commander will, insofar as possible, build up his plan of organization and action in such manner as to incorporate as much of the offensive theory of operation as the situation will permit. This general underlying principle of German employment of troops and matériel should always be kept in mind in connection with the following discussion, which in accordance with the above classification has been divided into a section covering the use of AA with forces in the field and a section covering the use of AA in Germany and other static defense areas.

12. GENERAL PRINCIPLES

a. The German Task Force

A German general has stated that the real secret of the initial success of the German Arms was "the combined employment of all arms on the battlefield in pursuance of one common mission." Related to this statement is the German conception of a task force as a grouping of the necessary arms and services, under one commander, for the accomplishment of a definite specified mission. Use of the task force implements another basic principle of command: that for a given mission a commander is selected, given the means, and allowed to carry out the assignment unhampered.

b. Antiaircraft Task Force Allocation

Following the general principle, AA artillery is assigned to specific task forces by the German High Command in accordance with the estimated need for AA artillery in execution of the mission. The size and composition of the AA artillery units so assigned will depend on several considerations, the most important of which are as follows:

> The mission (and its importance);
> The amount and characteristics of enemy aviation;
> The amount, types, and characteristics of friendly aviation available;
> The commander's estimate of the means required;
> The amount and type of AA artillery matériel available;
> The terrain;
> Proximity to the enemy;
> The weather and the season of the year.

c. Primary Missions of AA

In general, the primary missions of the AA artillery are considered by the Germans to be as follows:

Defense against hostile aerial reconnaissance;
Defense against hostile artillery observation;
Defense against hostile air attacks on personnel and important installations;
Support of friendly air combat strength.

Light, medium, and heavy AA weapons supplement each other in their effect. While the light and medium AA weapons furnish protection against low-flying hostile aircraft, the heavy weapons bear the brunt of the AA defense in the combat zone, combining long range with rapid fire and mobility.

The main mission of the heavy AA guns is to protect the ground against air reconnaissance and high-altitude attacks while on the march, at rest, or in actual combat. Moved by tractor or truck, the average marching speed of these heavy AA guns is from 5 to 20 miles per hour. Horse-drawn AA cannon are employed only by units contending with fuel shortages or very unsuitable road nets. Antiaircraft units moved by tractor or truck can be prepared for action rapidly; they have great mobility, and can be employed within the effective range of hostile artillery.

d. Transition from AA Role to Other Roles

In the approach to battle, as contact is made with the enemy, the German task force commander will utilize all facilities under his control to gain control of the air. For this purpose, he will employ all the aircraft at his disposal. During this same phase AA artillery will be employed in its primary mission of ground defense against hostile aircraft.

As control of the air is achieved, there is a transition in the employment of the ground arms. In direct proportion to the completeness achieved in control of the air, AA artillery becomes available for other missions. Since AA artillery guns combine the advantages of high mobility, high muzzle-velocity, accurate and rapid firing methods, and a flat trajectory, they are used against tanks and armored vehicles once their need in an AA role has become secondary.

While acting in their primary role, AA weapons will be employed against tanks, armored vehicles, or other ground targets only as a means of self-defense, or under circumstances where principles of surprise fire may apply. Since AA artillery is used by the Germans quite extensively to protect field artillery installations against hostile aircraft during the early phase when air control is being established, AA units in performance of this mission often find themselves in forward areas, and their very existence frequently depends on the ability to engage hostile tanks and armored vehicles.

Experiments with the use of AA guns (especially the 88-mm in the Spanish Civil War), together with later practical experiences in the Battle of France, resulted in AA weapons being mounted so that they could be used against ground as well as air targets. The 88-mm gun is the best example of this development, and its use in Russia against heavily armored vehicles was so successful that it began to be used more and more in a separate antitank role. This role has received much publicity and attention, but it should not obscure the fact that on most occasions the primary mission of the 88-mm gun is against hostile aircraft.

13. OPERATIONAL USE AGAINST AIR TARGETS

a. General

It is a frequently repeated axiom in the German Army that every combat unit is responsible for its own AA defense against low-flying aircraft. Every man armed with a rifle is trained to use it against such aerial targets, it having been found that concentrated fire by rifles is very effective against attack by low-flying or strafing planes, up to slant ranges of about 500 yards. Machine-gun fire is considered effective up to about 800 yards; light- and medium-caliber AA cannon, up to a slant range of about 2,000 yards. Heavy AA artillery is considered as being effective for fire up to about 9,000 yards, but is not generally considered as being available for use against planes flying directly over the battery at altitudes of less than 400 yards. For this reason each heavy battery is supported by two 20-mm AA cannon, which are an organic part of the battery organization. Figure 15, which is taken from an authoritative German military manual used extensively by German junior officers, gives an analysis of the slant ranges of responsibility for defense against enemy aerial targets. It should be noted, however, that the maximum slant ranges shown in the figure are less than the actual maximum capacities of the weapons concerned.

b. Protection of Columns on the March

(1) *Panzer divisions.*—German Panzer divisions on the move are trained to keep a considerable distance between separate units and groups, and where possible

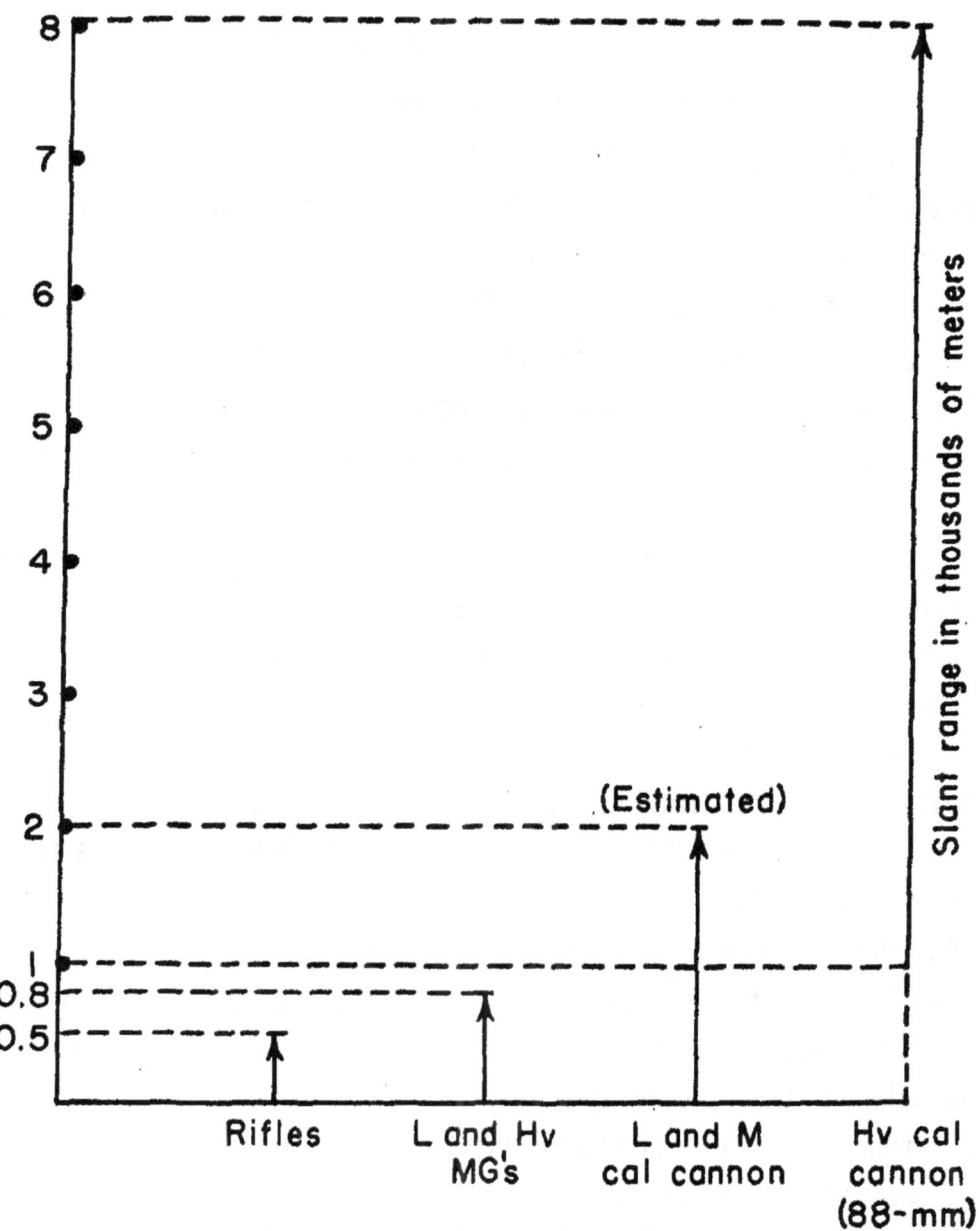

Figure 15.—Slant-range chart.

the division generally marches in several columns along parallel roads. Usually the majority of AA guns will be found well forward in the columns, and all defiles, bridges, and stopping places will be well defended by AA units. The columns usually halt after 2 hours for

20 minutes' rest, and after 4 or 5 hours' movement a halt of at least 3 hours is normal.

In the event of air attack, the column continues its march, and machine guns and the light and medium AA gun crews open fire. If the air attack proves to be of such weight that casualties to truck-borne troops will be severe, the column halts and the troops take cover. The drivers, however, remain with their vehicles. When air attack threatens in open country, the tank columns deploy in open formation, usually V-shaped.

(2) *Other units.*—As mentioned above, all German troops are trained to use their rifles and machine guns for mass fire-power against low-flying and strafing airplanes, while on the march as well as in other situations. Antiaircraft artillery units, both organic *Heeresflak* units and attached Luftwaffe AA units, furnish the necessary AA protection in essentially the same manner as when operating with armored divisions, the only difference being that slower-moving units and supply echelons may require a special type of defense. It should also be remembered that, in cases where the AA artillery is defending supply echelons, AA emplacements along prescribed routes of supply may be more or less static in nature.

c. Use in Forward Areas with Attacking Units

(1) *General.*—The use of AA units attached to Army divisions and corps will vary with the situation and in accordance with the higher commander's views as to how the AA artillery under his control can best be used in carrying out his attack mission.

(2) *Example of use with an attacking Panzer division.*—An order of the 15th Panzer Division, dated May 25, 1942, gives an interesting insight into the divisional commander's employment of the AA forces at his disposal. The order is for the assembly of the division in preparation for an attack. The 15th Panzer Division occupied a central position, the 90th Light Division being on the right and the 21st Panzer Division on the left. The 15th Panzer Division was organized into four groups as follows: an armored group, a reconnaissance group, a supporting group, and an infantry group mounted on trucks.

(a) *Disposition of AA forces.*—The AA forces at the disposal of the 15th Panzer Division by this order consisted of—

   (1) An AA battalion staff;
   (2) One heavy AA battery (6 heavy and 2 light guns),
   (3) One light AA battery (12 light guns),
   (4) One light AA battery, less one section (9 light guns);
} Luftwaffe AA troops

   (5) One AA company (12 light guns) of organic *Heeresflak* troops.

These forces were distributed as follows:

                                      Allocated to

(1) AA battalion staff_____ Staff of 15th Pz Div (in the supporting group).

(2) Heavy AA battery_____ 8th Tk Regt (in the armored group). Prior to the commencement of the operation, the heavy AA battery was ordered to protect the assembly against air attack.

(3) Light AA Battery (12 light guns):

	Allocated to
Battery staff and 1 section (3 light guns).	Field artillery and engineers of the armored group.
One section (3 light guns).	Field artillery of the supporting group.
One section (3 light guns).	Heavy AA battery ((2) above) for local defense against low-flying aircraft.

(4) Light AA battery, less 1 section (9 light guns):

Battery staff and 1 section (3 light guns).	AA battalion staff (in the supporting group).
One section (3 light guns).	Engineers of the supporting group.
One section (3 light guns).	Staff of the 15th Pz Div.

(5) AA Company (12 light guns):

Company staff and 2 sections (8 light guns).	Mounted infantry group.
One section (4 light guns).	Reconnaissance group.

(b) *Analysis of dispositions.*—The following points of interest arise from an analysis of the order and the above dispositions:

(1) The chain of command is from the AA battalion staff (attached to the staff of the Panzer division), through the heavy and light battery staffs with the armored group and the light battery staff with the support group.

(2) The heavy battery is seen in a dual role. In the approach to battle it provides AA protection; it turns to the ground role in support of the tanks when battle is joined.

(3) The light batteries protect the divisional and AA battery staffs, the field artillery, the engineers, and the heavy AA battery against low-flying attack. The ground role is secondary.

(4) The organic AA company gives protection against low-flying attack to the mounted infantry and reconnaissance groups.

(5) The forces mentioned in the orders of the 15th Panzer Division do not comprise an entire mixed AA battalion, the missing elements being two heavy batteries and one section of a light battery. In this connection, it is known that a considerable force of heavy AA guns (no doubt accompanied by a few light guns for close protection) was operating as an independent antitank group in this operation, and the missing elements of the battalion were undoubtedly assigned to the separate ground-target mission.

d. Protection of Rear-Area Installations

In operating with task forces, certain of the attached AA units are allotted for protection of Army and Air Force installations. Even in moving situations, AA must be designated to defend important semipermanent installations such as depots, parks, railheads, bridges, airdromes, etc. No hard-and-fast set rule is laid down for this use of AA artillery. The size of the AA force defending such areas will depend to a large extent on the AA artillery which is available for this assignment. Another consideration is whether or not superiority of air power has been attained.

Employment of the available AA forces will vary. In the western campaign in May, 1940, the AA defense of the German forces in the main attack over the Meuse River from Dinant to Sedan remained in the hands of an AA corps commander. The AA corps was composed of a number of AA divisions, each organized into regiments and separate battalions. Once the crossing was affected, the AA units comprising the corps were attached to other forces advancing on their missions. In later stages of that campaign, it was customary for the AA artillery to protect forward elements by attaching one battalion of three 88–mm gun batteries to each army corps, and one battalion of the same size to each army.

e. Defense of Railway Trains

(1) *General.*—The mounting of AA matériel on railway mounts for the protection of railway trains and as a means of furnishing a mobile defense of lines of communication has been highly perfected by the Germans. It should be noted that AA guns mounted on railway mounts can be used either in rear areas for protection of trains operating therein, or for the protection of trains carrying troops or supplies to forward combat areas. For example, the Germans use these mounts for the protection of important trains operating in Germany, but they also have had these mounts in large numbers throughout Russia during the Russian Campaign. Although the 20-mm Flak single- or four-barreled gun is normally employed, it is known that the 37-mm, the 88-mm, 105-mm, and possibly the 75-mm and 150-mm Flak guns are also used for this purpose.

(2) *Method.*—A German manual lays down certain

rules for employment of AA guns on railway mounts. A flatcar known as the *R-Wagen* is the truck prescribed by the German manual for use with the 20-mm gun. The gun is mounted on one end of the car. The crew is carried under a removable roof on the other end. Safe defenses are put up around the gun for "safe" firing zones. The manual prescribes three general methods in which protection may be given to trains:

> Three cars mounted with a machine gun on AA mounts and situated respectively one-fourth, one-half, and three-fourths of the way along the train;
>
> Three trucks carrying 20-mm light Flak guns, one in the middle of the train, one at the rear, and one immediately behind the locomotive. The gun behind the locomotive is usually not manned, being a spare to permit reversing the train without shunting the guns.
>
> On especially important trains an additional 20-mm gun may be carried on a truck in front of the locomotive.

On the move, the guns are continuously manned, priority areas of 180 degrees being allotted as follows:

> Forward: To the front machine gun and the center 20-mm Flak guns;
>
> Rearward: To the center and rear machine guns, and the rear 20-mm Flak guns;
>
> Forward: To the 20-mm Flak gun (when carried) in front of the locomotive.

These means of defense of railway trains are not

necessarily the only ones possible, as it is known that the position (or sequence of the positions) of AA guns protecting the trains may be changed at any time to comply with particular requirements.

Since care must be taken that the AA guns are not struck by obstructions such as passing trains, tunnels, signal posts, etc., lookouts are detailed to observe on each side of the train. When not firing, the 20-mm guns are pointed directly to the front or rear depending on their sector of fire.

Since no warning of attacks can be expected, all AA personnel must be kept in a constant state of readiness. There are two aircraft watchers, one observing an arc of 180 degrees to the front, the other to the rear. These watchers are selected from among the best-trained men and relieved frequently.

When the train is moving, where possible only tracer ammunition is used, since the motion does not permit accurate sighting. Care is taken not to shoot up signal posts and other installations, and where there are overhead powerlines, no firing is done even under attack.

f. Searchlights

Searchlight units consisting of heavy searchlights are normally assigned to task forces only in those cases where the assigned mission may require their use. With field forces engaged in offensive operations, the employment of heavy searchlights will be rare. Their use would normally be confined to rear areas, under circumstances where the situation has become static and it is necessary to employ heavy AA protection. Inasmuch as light searchlights are an organic part of the light AA battalions, a certain number of light searchlight batteries will be found moving into forward areas with the field forces. As their use will be limited, however, the tendency of German commanders is to leave the bulk of the searchlights in rear-area positions for defense of those areas. As these light searchlight batteries are highly mobile, it should be remembered that the commander can also use them in a variety of ways other than against aircraft, such as defense against parachute troops and in night ground attacks.

g. Antiaircraft Warning System

For warning against hostile aircraft both in the field and in rear areas, the Germans have a troop-warning service of the AA artillery which is similar in principle to the Antiaircraft Artillery Information Service (AAAIS) of U. S. AA units. Every active German AA unit observes the air in the area under its jurisdiction with specially trained personnel known as air guards. Through a system of communication facilities, these air guards submit detailed reports of hostile aircraft in their vicinity. Under normal circumstances the AA battalion headquarters is responsible for forwarding appropriate warning reports to the air-arm commander at higher headquarters.

14. OPERATIONAL USE AGAINST GROUND TARGETS

a. General

The basic principle of German combat methods has said to be a clever adaptation of fire to movement, with fire power increasing directly in proportion to the resistance encountered. Movement is normally from one piece of advantageous terrain to another, with maximum fire applied during the movement. Both fire and movement are applied with one basic purpose in view: to attain the objective of the unit. This principle is applicable to the offensive combat of all German units, from squads to armies.

In defense the German commander chooses the most suitable ground for combined action by infantry, machine guns, antitank guns, artillery, and tanks. In such depth as resources permit, he will usually construct a series of defense areas capable of all-around defense against any form of attack. The artillery of all types will be placed where it can support either the defense area, or the tanks if these are launched in a counterattack. In withdrawals, after skillfully thinning out most of the transport facilities and battle impedimenta, the German commander will usually launch some form of feint action to cover the withdrawal of the remainder of the force. This feint action often takes place in the evening; during the night the whole force withdraws, leaving only reconnaissance elements supported by a few guns to hold up hostile forces. In any of the above general situations, full use in roles against ground targets can be expected to be made of any AA guns not specifically required for use in an AA role.

b. 88-mm Dual-Purpose Gun

(1) *In antitank roles.*—Using both HE and AP ammunition, the 88-mm Flak gun has been used o

fronts with deadly effect against medium and heavy tanks. Its worth as an AT weapon was proved in the Polish and French campaigns; since the beginning of the Russian Campaign, when it was used with much success against large Russian tanks the armor of which proved invulnerable to the then standard German 37-mm AT gun, the 88-mm gun has been considered by the Germans to be their heavy AT weapon.

Wherever balanced AT support is considered necessary, it is now considered usual for German task-force commanders to allot a certain proportion of 88-mm guns for purely AT roles. This is especially true since the weapon has made its appearance on the new 12-ton half-track vehicle, which is armored in front and carries a small supply of ammunition. When mounted on this self-propelled mount, the gun is used only for engaging ground targets, necessary AA protection being furnished from other sources. It should be remembered, however, that the gun can also be used in an AT role when mounted on the special trailer (No. 201), which is fitted with pneumatic tires and is drawn by a half-track vehicle carrying the gun crew and a small supply of ammunition. Such ground targets as tanks can be engaged while the gun is in this traveling position.

(2) *In other roles.*—Since German military commanders are trained to utilize all available weapons to a maximum degree, it is not at all surprising that this gun has been used in other than AA and AT roles. Thus, in the battle for Sevastopol in the Russian Campaign, the German command was confronted with a narrow front barricaded completely with concrete, steel,

and guns. In view of the mobility of the 88-mm Flak gun, an AA combat detachment manning one of these guns was ordered to support a local infantry attack. At short ranges and over open sights, this gun engaged pillboxes and other enemy centers of resistance which the infantry could not overcome, thus assisting the infantry in carrying out its mission.

In many sectors, this gun has been used in normal field artillery roles. It has been used against fortified bunkers as well as against personnel. In the crossing of the Albert Canal in the Western Campaign, it was used in a ground role to cover the bridging operations being carried on by engineers.

(3) *Fire-control methods.*—For use against armored vehicles, and for field artillery tasks, the following four methods of fire control have been used: direct fire, using a telescopic sight; director control; fire directed from an observation post; and air burst HE.

(a) *Direct fire.*—This has been the most successful method employed against armored vehicles. Apart from the extreme mobility of the gun, the efficient telescopic sight has contributed largely to the success of the 88-mm gun in an AT role. The latest mark of telescopic sight used is the ZF 20–E, which has already been described.

(b) *Director control.*—With director control, the data for the first round is calculated in the same manner as for an air target. Corrections for direction, range, and fuze range are made from observation of fire and arbitrarily set into the director. This method has not proved very satisfactory.

(c) *Fire directed from an OP.*—When the target is below the horizontal, or at ranges greater than 10,340 yards (i. e., beyond the limit of the telescopic sight), fire may be directed from an observation post. The OP officer takes azimuth, range, and elevation from his fire-control map. From these, he calculates the firing data with a range table and transmits the data to the gun position by telephone. A director is sometimes used for giving the initial direction to the guns. Corrections are ordered from observation of fire and are applied at the guns.

(d) *Air-burst HE.*—Fire for effect with time-fuze air-burst HE against troops in the open, and against battery positions, has also been reported. Ranging is carried out with a low height of burst. Fire for effect follows with the fuze range being adjusted to obtain the most effective height of burst. It is believed that this method is not used very often.

c. Light and Medium Flak Guns

(1) *In an antitank role.*—The light- and medium-caliber Flak guns (20-mm and 37-mm) have had less outstanding success against tanks and armored vehicles than has the 88-mm, owing undoubtedly to the fact that the smaller caliber somewhat limits their use. However, there is no question that with their extreme mobility and high rate of fire, and the penetrating effect of their AP shells, the smaller guns will continue to be used extensively in AT roles, particularly in emergencies.

(2) *In other roles.*—Aside from AT roles, light flak

weapons, particularly the 20-mm, have been used for many different purposes against ground targets. They have been used against hostile machinegun nests, and bunkers have been neutralized by using these weapons for attacks on the openings. They have been employed in occupied villages and towns to overcome scattered resistance, and, like the 88-mm guns, they have also given ground support to engineers engaged in bridging operations.

(3) *General.*—Fire control for all the above uses is by normal or telescopic sight, with observation of the tracer.

15. ESTABLISHMENT OF GUN POSITIONS

a. Heavy AA Guns

(1) *For primary AA role.*—In the normal battery of four heavy AA guns, the pieces are disposed roughly in a square of approximately 70 yards. A fully equipped battery position will have two command posts, but this may vary in accordance with the importance of the locality and the availability of fire-control equipment. There are also several types of six-gun layouts.

(2) *For other roles.*—Emplacement of the 88-mm gun when being used primarily against tanks or in a role other than AA depends partly upon the terrain and partly upon certain rules laid down for the selection of a firing position, as follows: the angle of impact should not be greater than 60 degrees; the range should generally not exceed 2,000 yards; the gun level should slope downward (since the gun level varies from $-3°$ to $+15°$ from the horizontal of the muzzle); the position should

be concealed, and as near to the target as possible in order to insure maximum accuracy and surprise in opening fire; the lanes of approach and withdrawal must be as firm, level, and wide as possible.

As both the four- and six-gun layouts used in forward areas do not differ materially from those prescribed for AA guns engaged in the defense of Germany and in other static rear-area positions, attention is invited to the discussion of this subject appearing in Section IV of this study.

b. Light and Medium AA Guns

Light and medium Flak guns are normally disposed in platoons of three. A triangular layout is common but not unchangeable, with the guns anywhere from 75 to 150 yards apart. These light guns are seldom deployed singly; however, in other than AA roles their use may depend primarily on emergency conditions, with consequent deviations from normal methods of disposition.

16. DECEPTION AND CONCEALMENT

Common German practice in all types of military operations, as enunciated in their field service regulations, calls for the maximum use of surprise, which in turn involves secrecy, deception, and speed of execution. During the early European campaigns of the present war, because of overwhelming initial aerial superiority, the Germans did not pay too much attention to the camouflage of AA positions and to other passive defense practices. In later and present campaigns, however, the Germans have not always had definite air superiority, and they have used many passive means of deception and concealment, such as camouflage and erection of dummy gun positions and objectives, to protect themselves from aerial observation and to assist in maintaining the secrecy of their dispositions and operations. In the Libyan Desert, much ingenuity has been shown in concealing AA weapons, especially through dummy gun positions. Vehicles as well as guns are camouflaged with nets and local material, and resort is had to as much dispersion as possible under the tactical circumstances. In one operation in July of 1941, German guns were located among abandoned Italian artillery which had been left there from previous battles. These guns were not noticed until they opened fire.[11]

---

[11] A further treatment of this subject may be found in the discussion of passive means of defense appearing in the following section.

Section IV. USE OF AA IN DEFENSE OF GERMANY AND REAR AREAS

17. HISTORICAL BACKGROUND

In the years immediately prior to Germany's entry into World War II, the Germans conducted many experiments and tests designed to produce satisfactory AA weapons. Even after the experiments conducted during the Spanish Civil War, and the consequent determination to commence extensive manufacture of dual-purpose AA/AT guns, the primary AA purpose of these guns was never lost sight of. The German press gave much publicity to the importance of AA guns in the defense of Germany, and the Government simultaneously proceeded to provide for the activation and equipping of AA units in unprecedented numbers. Since plans for employment of these AA units in defense presupposed close cooperation with aviation, the rapidly growing AA forces were made an organic part of the German Air Force. With the outbreak of war, the formation of new AA units for local defense as well as for field service proceeded apace.

18. GENERAL ORGANIZATION OF AA DEFENSES

a. Responsibility

In addition to his other duties, the Chief of the German Air Force is responsible for the defense of territorial Germany and of important installations and cities of the occupied countries. An inspector for each separate arm of the Luftwaffe (similar to our former chiefs of branches) functions directly under the Chief of the Air Force and is responsible directly to the Chief for the state of training and efficiency of the separate elements comprising the rear-area defenses.

b. Defense Districts

For the purpose of home defense as well as for other needs, Germany and the important occupied territories are divided into air territorial areas known as *Luftgaue*. In 1939, 15 of these air territorial districts lay within the borders of Germany. In addition, there were two separate air territories established for areas especially open to hostile air attacks. These comprised the Air Defense Zone, West, which was almost identical with the area covered by the West Wall fortifications, and the Air Defense Zone, Sea, which covered in general the North Sea coastal and island area. Following the French Campaign, the first zone was eliminated. Other *Luftgaue* were organized within the occupied countries, however, to tie in with the general scheme of defense against air attacks.

The commander of a *Luftgau* is subordinate to the Chief of Air Forces alone. Even though his *Luftgau* may correspond in extent and nomenclature to a geographical army corps area, he is in no way subordinate to the army corps area commander. The *Luftgau* commander may have been originally an air officer or an AA artillery officer, or even an air signal officer. There is no rule on the matter other than that he must be an Air Force officer.

Luftgaue coordinate their defenses with each other, in accordance with regulations published by the Chief of the Air Force. The commander of the individual *Luftgau* has specialists who act respectively as commanders of the interception, pursuit, and other aviation; commanders of all AA artillery of the district, including searchlights; and commanders of the signal service employing warning and communication facilities. Other specialists, functioning directly under the district commander, include the commanders of barrage balloon units and of units responsible for carrying out so-called passive-defense measures. The operating units function under the specialist commanders both on direct orders from these commanders, and, when occasion demands, upon the initiative of the unit commander. In actual operations, in most cases the commands above the actual operating units act mainly in a coordinating capacity, feeding information to the operating units who act in turn on their own initiative in accordance with prescribed standing operating procedure.

Within certain of the air districts there are special air defense commands. These cover regions of vital importance whose defense must be insured with a maximum of defense facilities. In these defense commands, of which the cities of Berlin and Hamburg, and the Ruhr district, are typical examples, there are concentrated under a single command sufficient defense facilities of all kinds to prevent the attacking hostile air forces from carrying out their mission.

c. Component Arms

The AA guns are considered the backbone of the static defense, but the operation of the system calls for close cooperation with friendly aircraft, especially fighter planes. Searchlight units as a part of Flak proper play a very important part in the German scheme of air defense, and in certain areas barrage balloons are used quite extensively. The Aircraft Warning Service is a part of the Air Force, and as such has the mission of providing adequate warning of hostile aircraft. Certain passive measures form a very important part of the defense system as a whole; these measures must be considered a definite though intangible weapon, so closely tied in with the entire defense system that they must be considered in this discussion.

19. THE AA COMMAND IN AN AIR DISTRICT

a. Groups and Sub-Groups

The Flak, or AA, command in an air district is divided into "Groups" known as *Flakgruppen*. The Groups in turn are divided into "Sub-Groups" called *Flakuntergruppen*. These types are ordinarily territorial divisions. For example, one of the large industrial cities of Germany is divided into two Groups known as the North and South Groups, and each of these in turn has two Sub-Groups. In addition, there is a Sub-Group for outlying territory east of this town, and one for the northwest approaches.

b. Control Centers

The control center of the Flak defenses is the Group. The Group operates downward through sector controls, which in most cases are the Sub-Groups. These sector controls are the operational headquarters for various purposes—such as, for example, for fire control involving the ordering of barrage fire. The sector control is also used as a communication center. Close liaison is maintained between the Flak organizations and the warning service, and between Flak and air fighter-interception units.

c. Operational Units

Operational units are the battalions, regiments, and higher units. Organization of the individual units above the battalion is not uniform, the exact composition of the unit depending upon the part which it is expected to play in the defense scheme. Thus regiments may be found which consist entirely of searchlight units, entirely of gun units, or even of two mixed gun battalions and one searchlight battalion (the prewar standard). Even batteries may vary in organization, as in the case of gun batteries where the fire unit is composed of six instead of four guns. Although the battalion (*Abteilung*) is considered the basic unit, the necessity of deploying batteries makes it impossible in most cases for the battalion commander to exercise detailed control, and the heavy gun battery is normally the fire unit.

20. EMPLOYMENT OF AA GUNS

a. Static Guns (fig. 16)

Guns emplaced on permanent mounts or in static positions are generally used throughout the air defense system. The emplacements are usually well prepared, with living quarters for the crews. Calibers of these static guns range from the light 20-mm to the heavy 150-mm guns, most of the latter being permanently emplaced in readiness for both AA and coast defense roles. It is known that the light- and medium-caliber guns are also mounted on the tops of high buildings and factories.

b. Use of Towers

Guns engaged in a static role are also emplaced in towers of various kinds. For example, in Berlin there are at least two concrete towers 250 feet square and over 100 feet high. Each of these has a "satellite" tower, a smaller rectangular structure about 350 yards distant. The larger towers each have four heavy AA guns, one being mounted on each corner; the smaller towers each have four light AA guns and what appears to be a radio-location instrument. It is believed that these towers are also used in the control system.

c. Use of Mobile Guns

Mobile guns include those on railway mounts. In some areas a proportion of the gun defenses are mobile so that guns and gun positions may be altered on short notice. In order to achieve the maximum effect, the Germans believe that the system of AA defense should

USE OF AA IN DEFENSE OF GERMANY 87

Figure 16.—German 88-mm gun in static position.
(Note protection provided for gun crew.)

be extremely flexible, and the active means of defense are therefore closely coordinated with the means for deception. Under this system, different positions can be taken by mobile units at different times. For example, if system "A" is used tonight, the mobile force will take position in area 1; if system "B" is selected, they will be installed in area 2, etc. These systems of antiaircraft defense are changed frequently in order to meet changes in the tactics of enemy aviation. The net result theoretically operates to produce confusion in the mind of any hostile aviator who might attempt to orient himself through locations of a series of gun positions based on past experience. Guns emplaced in these positions are nearly always countersunk to permit continuous firing throughout an air raid with maximum protection to the crews.

d. Use of Dummy Guns and Dummy Positions

In keeping with the practices of active deception mentioned in the previous paragraph, the Germans employ dummy gun positions and dummy guns. The latter are usually employed along probable lines of air approach, and it is known that dummy gun flashes have been used. Furthermore, mobile guns may rotate through the various dummy positions, thus precluding any safe conclusions, based on hostile air reconnaissance, as to the existence of a set system of dummy positions.

e. Disposition of AA Guns in Rear Areas

(1) *General.*—In heavily defended areas, heavy guns are disposed on the outskirts with special attention to the expected lines of approach. A certain number of

positions will be in the area itself, and will be situated about 6,000 yards apart where the target is a large one. Light guns are concentrated at particularly vulnerable points, such as factories and docks. They are occasionally emplaced on lines of approach, such as canals, rivers, or arterial roads. For isolated vulnerable points, the disposition of defenses is a special problem which varies with the nature of the particular target. For example, airdromes generally have 12 or more heavy guns, none placed nearer than 2 miles, and 12 to 30 light guns, none located nearer to the perimeter than 500 yards.

(2) *Heavy guns.*—(a) *Four-gun positions* (fig. 17).—In the normal four-gun layout, the guns are sited roughly in a square of approximately 70 yards to a side. A fully equipped position has two command posts, which for convenience may be termed Command Post No. 1 and Command Post No. 2. Command Post No. 1 is usually situated about 100 yards to the side of the gun layout, and contains the ***Kommandogerät,*** which transmits data by cable to a junction box located in the center of the square, and thence to each of the four guns. Command Post No. 2 is located approximately in the center of the square, and normally contains the auxiliary predictor (director), with its separate height- and rangefinder. Communication from the auxiliary predictor to each gun is by telephone. The fire is normally controlled from Command Post No. 1; in the event of destruction or failure of the ***Kommandogerät*** or the transmission system, fire is controlled from Command Post No. 2.

Depending on the terrain, 20-mm guns are normally located between the gun layout and Command Post No. 1 in order to provide protection against low-flying aircraft.

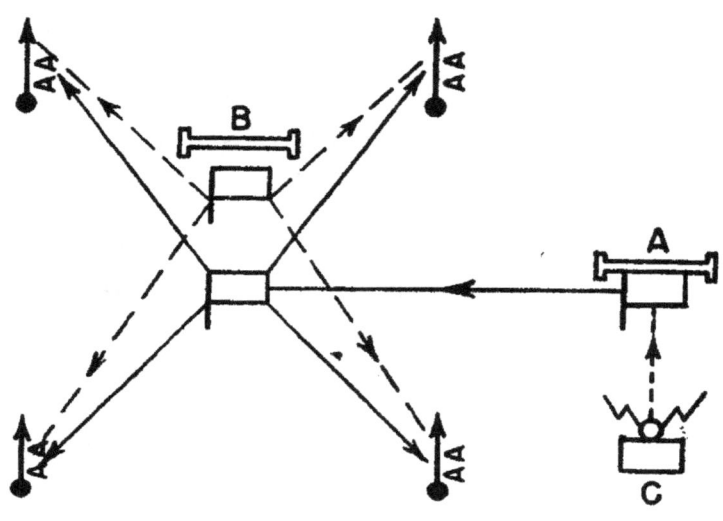

LEGEND

A — Command Post No 1 (with <u>Kommandogerät</u>)
B — Command Post No 2 (with <u>Kommandohilfsgerät</u>)
C — Radio-location set (where present)
——— Flow of electrically transmitted gun data
--- Flow of telephoned gun data

Figure 17.—4-gun layout.

In a great many cases, the normal four-gun layout has only one command post, either in the center or, more frequently, to the side. The provision of two command posts depends partly on the importance of the locality and partly on the availability of equipment.

It is interesting to observe that wherever the existence of radio-location fire control has been suspected or observed, the equipment has been found on sites with one command post to the side, and always in close proximity to the command post. Where this equipment is used, it is suspected that one set may furnish data for several nearby gun batteries.

(*b*) *Six-gun positions.*—Six-gun layouts fall into three main categories:—

(*1*) Those expanded from existing four-gun layouts by the addition of two emplacements, one on either side of the original square.

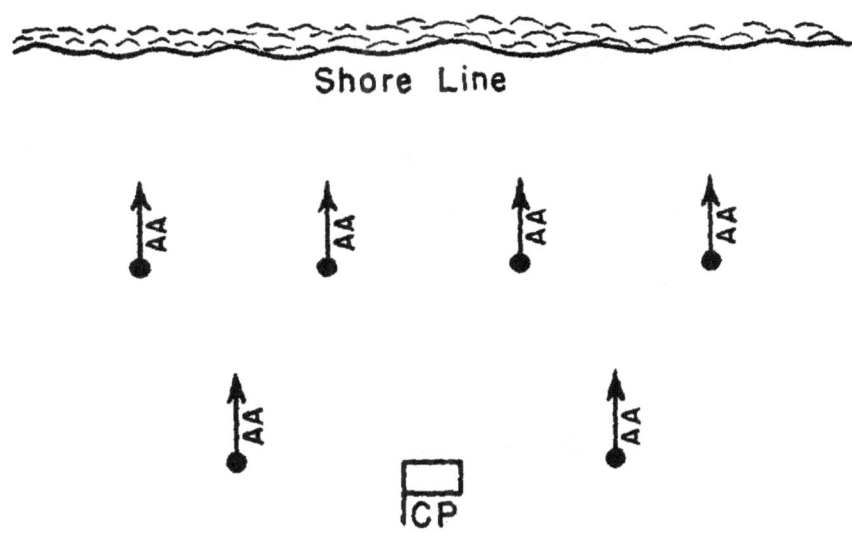

Figure 18.—6-gun layout for coastal defense.

(*2*) New layouts, consisting either of five guns sited roughly in the form of a circle, with the sixth gun in the center, or of all six guns in the form of a circle.

(*3*) Coastal layouts, consisting of four guns in a straight line facing the sea, with the remaining two guns in rear (fig. 18).

The command post on six-gun positions is almost invariably located outside the gun layout, except in the case of the coastal layouts, where it is usually located between the two landward emplacements.

(3) *Light and medium guns.*—A triangular layout of light and medium guns is common, but not invariable, with the guns anywhere from 75 to 150 yards apart. Guns are seldom deployed singly. In built-up areas, considerable use is made of light guns on specially constructed towers; they are also mounted on the roofs of buildings.

f. Fire-Control Methods

(1) *With heavy guns.*—The Germans use several types of fire-control methods with heavy AA guns. As has already been indicated, the data-computing director used by the Germans does not differ materially from that used by the U. S. Army, except for the fact that in the latest standard type of director the Germans incorporate the height- and range-finder and the predicting mechanism into one instrument. Since there are times when the target is not seen, or when for various reasons it may not be practicable to rely on fire directed at only one aerial target, the Germans use several methods of fire control, principally the following:

(a) *With director where target is seen.*—This is the normal method and is employed under suitable conditions by day, or in conjunction with searchlights by night. The use of mechanical fuze-setters permits the maintenance of a high rate of fire. Guns may fire singly, but in recent months a tendency towards salvo firing has been observed. At night, targets in searchlight "cones" are engaged by large gun densities, indicating a preference for this type of fire.

(b) *With director where target is unseen.*—This method may be used by day in overcast conditions, or by night in the absence of searchlight illumination. The use of this method presupposes some means, other than visual, of obtaining the basic elements of present azimuth, present angular height, and present slant range. The Germans are known to have experimented with and used searchlight sound locators for this purpose, fixing the location of the target in space by finding the intersection point of data received from two or more separate sound locators. Authentic reports indicate, however, that the Germans have not found the use of searchlight sound locators to be very satisfactory for this purpose. Since the Germans are known to have been employing radio-location instruments since 1940, it is quite certain that such instruments are now being used for obtaining the initial data.

(c) *Predicted concentrations.*—In this method a number of gun positions operate under a central control or "master station"; gun densities may include as many as 32 guns. Predicted salvos from individual positions have also been encountered. Unless irregular evasive action is taken by the hostile aircraft, both types of fire can be fairly accurately produced by taking a mean of plots of the plane's course.

(d) *Fixed barrages.*—This method was particularly used in the early part of the war. Controlled by a central operations room, the fire can be laid in almost any shape; screen, box, cylindrical, or in depth. This type of barrage is usually put up over a vulnerable point or just outside the bomb-release line. At the present time it is used mostly at night or under conditions of bad visibility. Furthermore, the development of up-to-date instruments has made its use secondary.

(2) *With light and medium guns.*—(a) *At visible targets.*—By use of the several course and speed sights, AA fire from light and medium guns is opened with reasonable accuracy, and corrections are made by observation of tracers. The light or medium AA guns are highly maneuverable and can engage a target almost immediately as it comes in view and in range. These guns rely for effect on the high rate and volume of fire. For altitudes below 1,500 feet, they are exceedingly accurate. At very low levels, particularly from 0 to 50 feet, accuracy is considerably reduced, owing partly to the limitation of field of view with a consequent restricted time of engagement, and partly to the high angular velocity of the target in relation to the guns. By night the method of engagement of an illuminated target is similar to that used by day, with greater reliance placed on observation of tracer.

(b) *At unseen targets.*—Against unseen targets, light AA fire is nothing more than a deterrent, as the Germans have no instruments for "unseen" firing with light and medium guns. These guns are sometimes sited close to a heavy searchlight, probably for the purpose of obtaining early approximate data, as well as for the protection of the searchlight.

(c) *Fixed or curtain barrages.*—Fixed or curtain barrages are occasionally fired by the weapons by day or by night over small vulnerable points, at targets or along likely lines of approach.

21. EMPLOYMENT OF SEARCHLIGHTS

a. General

The Germans use a large number of searchlights in connection with the AA defense of Germany and important installations of occupied countries. The searchlights have not been particularly successful in illuminating high-flying hostile bombardment planes at night for the sole benefit of gun units. The Germans have learned, however, to use their searchlights for other purposes. Searchlight crews are known to have been dipping their light beams to indicate to their fighter planes the direction in which hostile bombers are flying. Searchlights have also been used successfully to produce "dazzle" and "glare" in efforts to blind and confuse hostile pilots, bombardiers, and gunners. There is now no doubt that all these uses are proving a big help to the Germans in protecting their cities and strategic centers.

b. Equipment

As has already been indicated, the main searchlight equipment used by the Germans consists of the 150-cm (heavy) and the 60-cm (light) searchlights. The latter type is primarily for mobile employment with light Flak batteries. In addition to these two main items of equipment, the Germans also have a limited number of 200-cm and a few French 230-cm lights which are used to supplement the main equipment. Except for mass employment, initial data for the heavy searchlights are usually obtained through the use of sound-locators. With the development of radio-location equipment, there may now be a special set for use with searchlights, but no exact data is available on the extent of development in this field. It should be noted that the light searchlights use no sound locators, picking up their targets by definite searching patterns.

c. Location of Searchlights

Searchlights may be laid out in belts or in concentrations on likely lines of approach to important targets, and around or near gun-defended areas. German searchlights are used to aid night-fighter interception, and those at or near gun target areas are also used to cooperate with Flak. In gun-defended areas, searchlights are used to illuminate aircraft for Flak and for dazzle effect. The spacing of searchlights is as follows:

(1) *In belts.*—A belt usually consists of 10 to 15 or 20 to 30 searchlights, 1,000 to 2,000 yards apart along the course of the belt. The remainder of the lights are 5,000 to 6,000 yards apart.

(2) *In concentrations.*—When used in this manner, searchlights are usually spaced 2,000 to 3,000 yards apart in the shape of a triangle, a circle, or two concentric circles.

(3) *In gun-defended areas.*—Normal disposition is an even spacing approximately 3,000 to 4,000 yards apart. In some special areas, there are small groups with searchlights not more than 1,500 yards apart.

d. Searchlight Tactics

(1) *On cloudy nights.*—Unless a hostile airplane breaks through low-hanging clouds, only a limited number of searchlights, in belt or otherwise, go into action.

They attempt to follow the course of the aircraft along the base of the clouds in order to indicate its course to fighters or in order to produce an illuminated cloud effect against which the aircraft might be silhouetted for the benefit of fighters or the AA artillery.

(2) *On nights with considerable ground or industrial haze.*—When the searchlight beams are unable to penetrate the haze, searchlights occasionally go into action at a low angle of elevation on to the haze. They thus diffuse and produce over the target area a pool of light through which the crews of attacking aircraft find identification and orientation extremely difficult.

(3) *On clear dark nights.*—When in belts to aid fighter interception, the most usual functions are: to illuminate the target; to permit a limited degree of searching in "cone" formation; and, by exposing vertically, to produce ahead of the hostile bomber a wall of light against which it may at some time be visible to fighters attacking from the rear, or to compel the hostile bomber, as it runs the gantlet of lights, to fly so close to one of the beams or group of beams that it becomes visible from the ground, thus enabling other lights to engage. In the parts of belts where the lights are more openly spaced, some beams act as pointers for the benefit of night fighters.

In gun-defended areas, some groups of searchlights produce the maximum degree of dazzle, by exposing (almost vertically) and dousing at fairly regular intervals, and even by waving about in the sky.

Other groups of searchlights possessing a "master" light cooperate with Flak. If illumination is obtained, the guns engage; if not, fire is sometimes directed at the point of intersection of the beam over the target area or just outside the bomb-release line, beams being held stationary until a suitable target presents itself.

(4) *On clear moonlight nights.*—This condition greatly reduces the efficiency of the searchlights. In target areas, tactics are adopted similar to those employed on a clear dark night, except that less attention is paid to dazzle. When attempted, this method has not been able to prevent crews from bombing accurately. In belts, tactics are similar to those employed on a clear dark night, except that a larger number of lights are detailed to indicate the course of hostile aircraft.

e. Dazzle and Glare

"Dazzle" is the blinding of persons in a plane caught in the direct light rays of one or more searchlights. "Glare" means obscuring the target from the plane crew by a light beam played between the plane and the target.

The extent of dazzle is dependent on the height of the plane, the number of searchlights concentrated on it, weather conditions, the direction of the light beams, and to some degree on the reactions of persons in the plane.

Dazzle or glare created by AA searchlights greatly lowers the ability of an aviator to adapt his eyes to seeing at night. Either dazzle or glare makes the location of targets difficult and lessens the accuracy of bombing. Also, keeping beams directly on a plane helps defending fighter-craft to approach the plane unobserved and to attack it more effectively.

22. EMPLOYMENT OF BARRAGE BALLOONS

Although extensive use of barrage balloons was not planned by the Germans prior to commencement of World War II, very early in the war they made their appearance in certain industrial and strategic towns in western Germany.

The number of balloons in use varies with the considered needs of the area to be defended. For example, they are used in such large numbers over one of the important industrial regions of Germany that a recent observer reported that they were so thick that he "could see several hundred of them at one glance." Although the statement is undoubtedly far-fetched, it well illustrates the psychological value, aside from the practical value, that balloon barrages have.

According to reports, the German balloon barrage usually forms an irregular belt about five-eighths of a mile wide and about 1¾ miles from the outer edge of the target area. There is reputedly anywhere from 200 to 800 yards between the balloons. The balloons are flown at varying heights at different times, the exact height and numbers of balloons flown depending on the time of day, the weather, and the threat of aerial attack.

The purpose of the balloon barrage is to form an irregular pattern of perpendicular steel cables in the vicinity of the defended area, presenting a real as well as a mental hazard to any hostile aviator attempting to fly below the level of the balloons. The net result is to discourage hostile flyers from entering the region of the barrage for dive-bombing tactics against the defended area, and to force the hostile planes to an altitude less favorable for precision bombing. The plan for a barrage is coordinated with light-, medium-, and heavy-caliber gun defense, any gaps in the barrage being covered by light and medium Flak. It should also be noted that in defended areas which include harbors and docks, the balloon barrage may extend out over the water, balloons being suspended from stationary or movable barges.

23. AIRCRAFT-WARNING SYSTEM

a. Responsibility

The aircraft-warning service for Germany and for the important occupied areas is the responsibility of the German Air Force, and is a definite integral part of the organization of defense against hostile aircraft. Although a part of the Air Signal Service, for all practical purposes the aircraft-warning service is a separate organization created for the sole purpose of constant observation of the air space over Germany, and for the prompt recognition and reporting of airplanes flying over Germany and other defended zones of the interior. This service is operated through the air district headquarters commanders, to whom the aircraft-warning service is subordinated.

b. Operation

In the operation of this system, there is a fixed "German territorial aircraft-warning service," as well as a mobile aircraft-warning service which is carried out by "aircraft-warning-service companies."

The fixed "aircraft-warning-service net" is mesh-like in character. The distances of individual air guard lines from one another vary between 20 and 45 miles, these distances and lines being established in accordance with tactical considerations. "Air guard stations" comprising observation and reporting stations are generally 6 to 8 miles apart. "Air guard headquarters," comprising plotting and relaying stations, are agencies of the aircraft-warning service. As with our system, the function of the air guard stations is to report the number, type, height, flying direction, identity, etc., of any planes flying over the sector. These reports find their way to a center where they are filtered and evaluated, with subsequent disposition of appropriate information to military authorities as well as to civil protection authorities.

The motorized aircraft-warning companies supplement and increase the density of the fixed aircraft-warning net, as well as being put around a temporarily vulnerable area. Although ordinarily used well forward, they may be employed on open flanks and in rear areas.

The reports of the territorial aircraft-warning service are made by telephone and wire, whereas the reports of the motorized aircraft-warning companies are made by radio.

c. Flak Intelligence Service

The aircraft-warning service is supplemented by the troop-warning service of the German AA artillery, which is similar to the U. S. Antiaircraft Artillery Information Service (AAAIS). Every active German AA unit observes the air in the area under its jurisdiction with specially trained personnel. In addition, all troop units use their own air guards to avoid surprise. The guard gives warning by means of calls, horns, sirens, or blinker lamps.

d. Use of Radio-Detection Devices

It is known that both long- and short-range radio-location instruments are now being used for warning purposes. The long-range instruments are located at intervals along the Western European coast for early warning purposes, and undoubtedly other sets of both long and short range are scattered in a net throughout rear areas to supplement visual observation.

24. PASSIVE MEANS

In the defense of rear areas, the Germans lay much stress on the use of passive means. These involve every feasible type of deception, including the extensive use of camouflage. No effort has been spared to change the appearance of important potential air objectives as completely as possible. In 3 years of war, the system has been developed to a very high degree of efficiency. AA artillery units cooperate in the system of passive defense by the use of movable defense forces, and through carefully considered gun and searchlight positions. The civil population is well disciplined, and blackout regulations are stringently enforced.

Obviously, it is impossible to conceal the general location of a large military objective such as an industrial city. The Germans recognize this fact, and their attempts to deceive their enemy accordingly include removal of the center of gravity of the defense of the area from the center of the objective area itself. At night this is accomplished largely through the use of searchlights. A hostile flyer will usually fly toward the center of the ring of illumination, since he will assume that the center of the objective should be in that area. Under the German system, the center of the ring of searchlights is accordingly placed to one side of the center of the defended area. Furthermore, the center of the searchlight defense may be moved from time to time, thus precluding any definite "fix" of the center of the searchlight defense with respect to the true objective. For daytime deception, camouflage will be used to a very large extent, no effort being spared to bring about the maximum results.

In line with the German belief that if a considerable portion of the enemy attack can be diverted to dummy objectives, the defense may be considered to have been quite successful, the Germans use complete systems of dummy objectives around their important military establishments. Some of these dummy objectives have been so successful that they have been bombed by hostile aviation many times over. Active means are used to assist the effectiveness of the faked objectives. For example, at night when hostile aircraft bomb the dummy objectives, personnel housed in nearby bombproof shelters will start large fires to cause further bombing attempts at the objectives, and to confuse the fliers as to the outcome of their mission. To increase the effect of reality, in many cases the dummy objectives may be protected by AA artillery. Captured matériel is often used for this purpose. Dummy objectives are also placed near the center of the searchlight perimeter.

The use of dummy gun positions has already been mentioned. When these positions exist, the mobile section of the active AA artillery defense may move in and out of them. The use of dummy flashes may intermingle with the firing of real AA guns, as a result of which the hostile flier secures a very incorrect picture of the true situation on the ground.

Some examples of the extent of the use of camouflage by the Germans will not be amiss. It is well known that Berlin has been extensively camouflaged, not only the city itself but also the outskirts. One example is that of the most important distinguishing landmark in Berlin, namely, the wide avenue running east and west through the city and called the "Axis." The pavement of this avenue has been sprayed with a dark green paint to blend with the trees in the *Tiergarten* (a large park), along the avenue and throughout the western section of the city. The Victory Monument (*Siegesäule*), in the center of a circle on the Axis, has been painted with a dull color so as not to reflect light. An overhead cover of wire matting, interwoven with green materials to resemble vegetation, covers the avenue for a considerable distance. The wire netting is about 18 feet high and is interspersed with artificial shrubs and trees. About every 30 yards, the coloring and texture of the greenery has been changed. To eliminate shadows, netting has also been hung from the sides at an angle of about 20 degrees.

To create an opposite effect—that is, to simulate a street where in fact there is none—wire netting has also been used. These dummy streets are frequently connected with the real ones, which then disappear into artificial woods. In one instance it is reported that a "woods" was created by fastening artificial sprigs about 1 foot high and about 1 to 2 inches apart to a wire net. Through these "woods" a system of "roads" was painted in brown on the mesh of the net.

Many important buildings in Berlin have been camouflaged by covering them with nets, and by placing artificial barns, farm buildings, and trees on the roofs. Small lakes have been covered by reed-like mats.

The extent of these camouflage efforts is a good indication of the lengths to which the Germans will go in carrying out large-scale efforts at deception. It may well be expected that no means will be spared to hide the real disposition of gun positions and vital areas.

Section V. CONCLUSIONS

From an analysis of the contents of this study, certain general conclusions concerning German AA artillery and its employment may be drawn. The most important of these conclusions follow:

1. The organization of German AA artillery units is extremely flexible. The exact composition and size of any AA unit may vary with the specific mission to be performed.

2. Although German AA artillery as an arm is an organic part of the German Air Force, there are some AA units which are organic to higher Army units and are considered as Army troops. These furnish AA protection to the Army units of which they are a part.

3. AA units assigned to an Army field force are subordinated operationally and for command purposes to the Army ground unit with which they are operating.

4. The principal German AA weapons are dual purpose AA and AT weapons which can be and are used in other roles as well.

5. In the approach to battle, and until air superiority has been obtained, German AA weapons which are actually assigned to an AA role remain in that role, except for purposes of self-defense against ground targets or where sudden opportunities for surprise fire against ground targets outweigh the necessity for AA protection. As air superiority is obtained, however, AA weapons are released for AT missions as well as for other roles against ground targets.

6. At the outset of an operation, depending on the considered need for such use, a certain number of AA guns may be assigned to AT or other artillery roles.

7. The Chief of the German Air Force is responsible for the air defense of Germany and the important areas of occupied countries. This responsibility is carried out through subordinate air territorial districts and special defense commands, all of which contain sufficient fighter aviation, AA artillery with searchlights and barrage balloons, and necessary aircraft-warning-service units to effect a carefully coordinated AA defense.

8. The outstanding feature of the German air defense is the coordination effected by unity of command. All of the means in any single air defense, including fighter aviation, AA artillery, warning services, and civil defense organizations are under one commander, who is alone responsible for the accomplishment of the mission.

www.ingramcontent.com/pod-product-compliance
Lightning Source LLC
Chambersburg PA
CBHW080518110426
42742CB00017B/3165